WORKSCRIPTS

WORKSCRIPTS

Perfect Phrases for High-Stakes Conversations

STEPHEN M. POLLAN • MARK LEVINE

WILEY
John Wiley & Sons, Inc.

Copyright © 2010 by Stephen M. Pollan and Mark Levine. All rights reserved.

Published by John Wiley & Sons, Inc., Hoboken, New Jersey.
Published simultaneously in Canada.

No part of this publication may be reproduced, stored in a retrieval system, or transmitted in any form or by any means, electronic, mechanical, photocopying, recording, scanning, or otherwise, except as permitted under Section 107 or 108 of the 1976 United States Copyright Act, without either the prior written permission of the Publisher, or authorization through payment of the appropriate per-copy fee to the Copyright Clearance Center, Inc., 222 Rosewood Drive, Danvers, MA 01923, (978) 750-8400, fax (978) 646-8600, or on the web at www.copyright.com. Requests to the Publisher for permission should be addressed to the Permissions Department, John Wiley & Sons, Inc., 111 River Street, Hoboken, NJ 07030, (201) 748-6011, fax (201) 748-6008, or online at http://www.wiley.com/go/permissions.

Limit of Liability/Disclaimer of Warranty: While the publisher and author have used their best efforts in preparing this book, they make no representations or warranties with respect to the accuracy or completeness of the contents of this book and specifically disclaim any implied warranties of merchantability or fitness for a particular purpose. No warranty may be created or extended by sales representatives or written sales materials. The advice and strategies contained herein may not be suitable for your situation. You should consult with a professional where appropriate. Neither the publisher nor author shall be liable for any loss of profit or any other commercial damages, including but not limited to special, incidental, consequential, or other damages.

For general information on our other products and services or for technical support, please contact our Customer Care Department within the United States at (800) 762-2974, outside the United States at (317) 572-3993 or fax (317) 572-4002.

Wiley also publishes its books in a variety of electronic formats. Some content that appears in print may not be available in electronic books. For more information about Wiley products, visit our web site at www.wiley.com.

ISBN 978-1-118-09757-1 (special edition with CD)

Printed in the United States of America.

10 9 8 7 6 5 4 3 2 1

Contents

Preface xi

Chapter 1   The New Workplace Environment 1

Chapter 2   Workplace Bombshells 13
Workscript 2.1   Meeting your new boss   18
Workscript 2.2   Meeting your new staff   22
Workscript 2.3   Explaining a restructuring   26
Workscript 2.4   Announcing a purchase or merger   28
Workscript 2.5   Announcing a relocation   30

Chapter 3   Death Sentences 35
Workscript 3.1   Terminating a company icon   42
Workscript 3.2   You're the icon being terminated   44
Workscript 3.3   Firing a friend   46
Workscript 3.4   Being fired by a friend   48
Workscript 3.5   Terminating someone close to
                  retirement   50

Workscript 3.6	Being terminated when close to retirement	52
Workscript 3.7	Terminating someone with a personal burden	56
Workscript 3.8	Being terminated when you have a personal burden	58
Workscript 3.9	Terminating someone, but asking them to remain available	60
Workscript 3.10	Being terminated, but asked to remain available	64
Workscript 3.11	Making an end run around your boss	66

Chapter 4 Employer Cost-Cutting 69

Workscript 4.1	Furloughing someone without pay	74
Workscript 4.2	Being furloughed without pay	76
Workscript 4.3	Turning a full-time employee into a part-timer	78
Workscript 4.4	Being asked to become a part-time employee	80
Workscript 4.5	Cutting an entire staff's pay	82
Workscript 4.6	Cutting an individual employee's pay	86
Workscript 4.7	Having your pay cut	88
Workscript 4.8	Increasing employee's hours but not pay	90
Workscript 4.9	Extending responsibilities without increasing pay	92
Workscript 4.10	Having your responsibilities increased but not your pay	94
Workscript 4.11	Reducing an employee's staff	96

Workscript 4.12	Having your staff cut	99
Workscript 4.13	Reducing an employee's budget	100
Workscript 4.14	Having your budget reduced	103

Chapter 5 On Bended Knee   105

Workscript 5.1	Responding to a raise request	112
Workscript 5.2	Requesting a raise	116
Workscript 5.3	Responding to a promotion request	118
Workscript 5.4	Requesting a promotion	121
Workscript 5.5	Responding to a budget increase request	124
Workscript 5.6	Requesting a budget increase	126
Workscript 5.7	Responding to a request for time off	128

Chapter 6 Managing Up   131

Workscript 6.1	Turning down an assignment	134
Workscript 6.2	Asking for relief from a project	138
Workscript 6.3	Asking for a deadline extension	140
Workscript 6.4	Breaking bad news to your boss	144
Workscript 6.5	Warning of potential client or customer problems	146
Workscript 6.6	Warning of potential vendor or supplier problems	148

Chapter 7 Getting Personal   151

Workscript 7.1	Asking employees to improve their appearance	154
Workscript 7.2	Asking employees to improve their hygiene	156

Workscript 7.3	Publicly putting an end to staff backstabbing	158
Workscript 7.4	Privately putting an end to staff backstabbing	160
Workscript 7.5	Confronting someone who's backstabbing you	162
Workscript 7.6	Confronting a sexual harasser	166
Workscript 7.7	Ending staff sexual harassment	168
Workscript 7.8	Refusing to cover up for a peer	170
Workscript 7.9	Ratting out a peer	172
Workscript 7.10	Putting an end to brownnosing	174
Workscript 7.11	Stopping a flirtatious employee	176
Workscript 7.12	Stopping a flirtatious peer	179
Workscript 7.13	Putting an end to staff gossiping	180
Workscript 7.14	Confronting a gossip	183
Workscript 7.15	Confronting an employee with a drinking problem	184
Workscript 7.16	Confronting a peer with a drinking problem	186
Workscript 7.17	Putting an end to Internet abuse	189
Workscript 7.18	Questioning an employee's expenses	190
Workscript 7.19	Defending your own expense report	193

Chapter 8 Looking Out for Number One — 195

Workscript 8.1	Delivering a critical performance review	200
Workscript 8.2	Defending your own performance from criticism	201

Workscript 8.3	Asking an employee for self-criticism	204
Workscript 8.4	Responding to requests for self-criticism	206
Workscript 8.5	Offering suggestions for professional development	208
Workscript 8.6	Responding to suggestions for professional development	210
Workscript 8.7	Asking for a networking meeting	214
Workscript 8.8	Explaining a career shift to an interviewer	216
Workscript 8.9	Negotiating a job offer when you're still employed	218
Workscript 8.10	Negotiating a job offer when you're unemployed	220
Workscript 8.11	Giving notice	222

Epilogue 227

Index 229

Preface

This book is, more than anything else, a survival map. The workplace of today isn't just different, it's dangerous. I describe it in some detail in Chapter 1, but to make that long story, short: The rules that used to serve as guideposts have crumbled; the practices and behaviors that were standard, have been thrown to the side of the road. Most of us feel anxious and angry, and with good reason. It is scary out there in the working world, whether you've 25 years on the job or are have just graduated college.

That's the bad news.

Here's the good news: There is a way to make it through this unknown territory and emerge in a better place.

It starts with understanding how the dynamics of workplace communications have changed and adapting your attitudes and behaviors to match the new reality. That's what I've tried to help you accomplish in the following pages.

The book is filled with a great deal of situation-specific advice; tactics for typical scenarios you'll encounter, if not every day, then at least every month in your working life. There are also a number of recurring strategies which you'll find running throughout the chapters.

But if there's one main lesson you need to absorb about workplace communication today, it's this: everyone is talking *at*, not *with* each other.

In years past there were chances to change peoples' minds and attitudes; opportunities to win others over to your point of view; times when you convince someone to modify their position. It might have required charm, subtlety, cunning, or flattery, but it could be done. Today, it's almost never possible. That's because everyone is looking out for number one. As a result, workplace communications today is more about posturing than persuading.

In the pages that follow I help you posture, or position yourself, to your best advantage, in every situation covered. My short-term goal, the one addressed in this book, is for you to achieve the best outcome possible in that scenario.

This book will arm you so that you may survive the worst workplace imaginable, as it gives you inordinate insight into management's reasoning and their fears.

There is a long-term answer: redefining yourself and behaving as a freelancer rather than an employee, even if you're on the payroll. But that's the subject for another book. Right now, we've just got to get through this uncharted territory in one piece.

Stephen M. Pollan

WORKSCRIPTS

Chapter 1

THE NEW WORKPLACE ENVIRONMENT

Forget everything you have ever learned about workplace communications. Ignore all the rules for office behavior you've followed for years. Throw away all the books you acquired in past decades on job interviews and networking. The world of work has been transformed in ways both large and small. In less than two years the workplace has undergone a shift that is as dramatic as the transition that happened when we moved from an agricultural to an industrial economy. A sea change has occurred and business has truly entered the twenty-first century.

The Great Recession of 2008 was the obvious tipping point for this transformation. However, in hindsight, it's a change that has been building for years, perhaps even decades. Optimists may hope it's only a temporary shift, a short-term symptom of a finite economic crisis, and that the world will soon return to the way it used to be. But it is realistic, not pessimistic, to accept that the economic crisis was the dawn of a new business world that will last for the rest of our working lives.

While this shift will impact every aspect of our money life, the most obvious day-to-day effect is in the way we communicate and relate to our fellow workers. Quite literally, the way we say things to each other in the workplace must be different now. That's because how we all think and feel about our jobs, our careers, our employers, our peers, and our employees has changed.

I've been closely examining workplace communications for more than two decades. My name is Stephen M. Pollan and I'm an attorney, career coach, and financial advisor in private practice in New York City. While my practice has always been holistic, treating the personal and professional needs of my clients as a single cohesive whole, much of my work for the past 10 years has centered on the workplace. That's because it has been, and continues to be, the arena in which my clients' greatest fears and troubles play out. Besides taking a comprehensive approach, another thing that has always separated me from other advisors is that I offer extremely pragmatic advice. I tell my clients exactly what I think they should do and say. My clients and I develop scripts for their problematic dialogues, planning exactly what to say and how to respond in whatever situation they face.

This pragmatism and my scripting approach led me to write a book called *Lifescripts*, offering advice on what to say in a variety of difficult business and personal scenarios. I took a graphic approach to each conversation, plotting it out with a flow chart that followed all the possible responses, counters, and variations. The original book and its graphical approach was so successful that it spawned a number of successful sequels and follow-up editions, focusing on additional scenarios. Up until recently, I had assumed that I'd addressed all the most common situations and offered scripts for every eventuality.

But then in 2008 the workplace changed forever, forcing me to rethink and revise all the office communications advice I'd been offering over the years.

It's easy, even tempting, to characterize the changes of 2008 in a negative way. Change of any form is often frightening. And the past almost always takes on a nostalgic glow, whether or not it is deserved. With so many of these changes resulting in job insecurity or loss, declines in income, and narrowed future options, the urge to bad-mouth the new environment is strong. But that's an impulse it would be wise to overcome. There are few less appealing coworkers than the chronic complainer. No one wants to work for a bitter boss. And disgruntled, "sad-sack" job seekers are simply never hired. The best thing to do, the only thing anyone can do that actually matters, is to deal with the workplace as it is now, however we might feel about it.

What are the elements of this new workplace environment?

- Face-to-face communication is rare.
- Jobs and careers have expiration dates.
- Short-term results are all that matter.
- Employees do not trust employers.
- Everyone's work future is uncertain.

Let's explore each of these in some detail.

Face-to-face communication is rare. The ubiquity and convenience of new electronic communications devices and formats have allowed everyone to be in touch with everyone else, 24 hours a day, almost anywhere in the world. We can send an e-mail from the summit of Mount Everest to someone in a New York City subway car, who can then forward it to someone else who is on an aircraft about to land in Dubai. Many people now prefer to communicate electronically, even if a more direct form of exchange is available. And the younger someone is, the more indirect most of his or her communications.

All of this electronic communication has unquestionably increased productivity and efficiency. But it has also had the unexpected consequence of making face-to-face communication much less common. The fewer chances we have to communicate face to face, the worse we get at it. Today many of us are more comfortable sending a text message with our thumbs than talking out a problem across a desk. One-on-one meetings are increasingly limited to only the most vital matters: such as hiring interviews, performance reviews, and terminations. As a result, during the most important communications of our working lives we're relying on skills we rarely practice anymore.

Jobs and careers have expiration dates. People used to lose their jobs because of personal conflicts, poor performance, or temporary economic conditions. You didn't get along with your new boss, so you were replaced. You weren't able to meet your sales quota, so you were fired. Or the company's revenues dropped, so you were laid off. These events were always frightening and difficult, and often unfair, but there were obvious ways to bounce back. You could find a job working for someone with whom you got along. You could improve your sales skills or find a product or service you were able to sell successfully. Or you could find a job with a company that was doing well, or wait and be rehired when business at your previous employer's company rebounded. However, today, people are being fired because their jobs have become extinct. And that means there's no hope of easy recovery.

While terminations still occur due to personal conflicts, poor performance, and temporary problems, the vast majority of employees today are losing their positions because of irresistible forces and inexorable societal trends. The first is the influence of information technology, which has impacted every industry, allowing tasks to be accomplished by fewer individuals. Whether it's producing a jet aircraft, a sweater, or a newspaper, fewer people are needed and, as a result, jobs are vanishing. The second trend is the move toward globalization. Technologically, logistically, and politically, borders are no longer the steep barriers they were before. Many of the jobs that haven't been eliminated by information technology can now be done at lower costs by employees working from their homes or from a remote location halfway around the globe. In today's workplace there's a natural, and entirely rational, sense that every job is temporary.

Short-term results are all that matter. In recent years, the leaders of most large businesses have changed the way they view finances and performance. Executive evaluations and compensation have become more closely linked to stock performance than to any other measure. Instead of rewarding leaders based on, say, the long-term growth and positioning of the company for the future, corporate boards and shareholders make their decisions and judgments based on how the stock fared for the quarter. Share prices almost always are linked to short-term rather than long-term measures. Exceed analysts' projections by a penny when a statement is released, and the stock climbs; fail to meet those projections by a penny, and the stock falls.

The obsession of corporate management with stock price has had a cascading effect on every other level of business hierarchy. With information technology allowing management to more closely and frequently track the performance of departments and individuals, employees are now expected to meet or beat projections and expectations on a quarterly or even monthly basis. Rather than being viewed as assets of the corporation, employees are now seen as being either revenue producers or as expenses. In either case, they are being judged on short-term results. Focusing on what is most expedient in the near future often has the unintended effect of harming future results. Robbing tomorrow for today almost always ensures eventual job extinction.

Employees do not trust employers. The concept of corporate loyalty has been dead for more than a generation. No one who has been in the workplace in the past two decades believes companies have any loyalty to workers. And at the same time, no rational employer has suffered under the illusion that an employee would remain loyal to the company unless it was in his or her own self-interest to do so. But while this lack of mutual loyalty was assumed and accepted, a degree of trust remained among employees toward the ethics of business. This residual faith was based on the notion that ability and performance would always be rewarded. Even if times were tough financially, and raises were impossible, employees believed that the smartest, most effective, and most productive among them would be the most secure. After all, wouldn't it be irrational for any company to fire its most productive workers? And yet, this one remaining belief has been shattered in the past two years, eliminating the sole thread of trust still linking employees to their employers.

Superior skill, knowledge, and productivity were no defense against termination during the Great Recession of 2008. Contrary to what every employee had believed, these traits often made it more likely for someone to be fired than retained. That was because the best employees were almost always the most highly paid employees. Faced with negotiating their way through dire straits, employers in paradigm-shifting numbers opted to give up productivity, because this sacrifice offered the greatest short-term expense cuts. Rationalizing that digital memory would compensate for the loss of institutional memory, employers fired their most experienced workers. The long-term impact of this is, and will continue to be, dramatic. If high performance is no longer rewarded and, in fact, turns the employee into a target, what motivation remains for someone to work hard or well?

Everyone's work future is uncertain. Separately, each of these four new elements of today's workplace is a game-changer. But taken together, they have combined to create a fifth element, one that's the most consequential of all. There is a near-universal feeling of uncertainty in the workplace. The future of everyone, from the CEO in the corner office to the security guard in the lobby, seems to be subject to change on a whim. The clear paths and expected patterns that we have all used as maps in our working lives no longer apply. Everyone feels cast adrift.

Before the Great Depression and World War II, when we lived in an agricultural and industrial society, most people followed predictable occupations. They found a trade to follow or a paying position and held onto it for as long as possible. They might get raises over time or shift jobs, but by and large their working lives were stable, if static. Since the end of World War II, most working lives have, in one way or another, followed a career path. It has been assumed that people would join the workforce in an entry-level position after acquiring some amount of education. As time passed and individuals gained knowledge and skill, they would move up in the hierarchy of their business, industry, or profession. Along with this increased ability, their incomes would rise as well. At some point, either because they ceased improving relative to other employees, or there was no opening above them, or there was no higher rung to climb to, they stopped moving up the ladder. However, their income would continue to climb, albeit at a slower pace, because seniority and experience were valued by the company. Then, when they reached the age of 65, they would retire from the workplace and rely on income from pensions, savings, and Social Security for as long as their golden years lasted.

With our national transition into an information age economy at the end of the twentieth century, this career model has slowly but surely been crumbling. The final collapse came with the Great Recession and the entirely new workplace it has left in its path of economic destruction. The expectation of an upward climb in responsibility and income, from entry into the workforce until retirement, is over. The age of the career is gone. We are now all employed in an ad hoc workplace in which excellence is no guarantee of security, let alone advancement; in which incomes could fall just as easily as climb with each new position; in which career changes will become the norm rather than the exception; and in which we may have to rely on earned income of one form or another for as long as we're physically and mentally capable of earning a paycheck.

What hasn't changed in this new ad hoc workplace is that you still have to engage in difficult dialogues. You still have to fire people with whom you're friendly. You still need to ask for raises and increased budgets. You still must put an end to office gossip and give performance reviews. You still have to break bad news to clients and defend your department's performance to your boss. No matter how different this new environment may be, you are still going to face all the vexing conversations of the past. And today they are even more problematic because of the changes that have taken place.

Let's look at the general changes created by this new environment.

With face-to-face communication much rarer now, we have fewer opportunities to hone our skills, not only at verbalizing, but at using our body language and facial expression to reinforce the spoken message we're trying to send. What once may have come as second nature now may require conscious effort. In addition, the partner with whom we're communicating is probably just as unpracticed at this as we are. That means their responses and reactions will be less predictable, requiring us to be a bit more nimble in our scripting.

The finite nature of every job means there's less investment, both emotionally and financially, in relationships to other workers, or to the company. There's less personal history to draw on in communications. In years past you were more likely to know what buttons to push with another party, or more important, what buttons *not* to push. Today almost every face-to-face dialogue is taking place between individuals who really don't know each other.

Since short-term results are all that matter, we are losing one previously valuable tool in our communication arsenal. Promises of future or potential events simply don't hold the value they did in years past. Appeals for patience now fall on deaf ears. Strategies that once made sense are apt today to require too much time to prepare or come to fruition. Time is no longer as valuable as money—it's more valuable.

The well-deserved lack of trust that employees have for employers today has done more than simply put an end to promises being accepted at face value. Employees approach conversations of any type with any representatives of higher management with skepticism. The assumption that, at the very least, the other party is being honest is gone. Verification and documentation are now required. Rewards deferred are perceived as being rewards denied, and also as signs of impending termination. The slightest failure to deliver on the part of management can generate a cataclysmic loss of morale and effort.

Finally, with everyone's future so uncertain, the workplace is a much tenser place that ever before. Nerves frayed during the Great Recession are going to remain so for the foreseeable future. Anger and fear are apt to be palpable. Short fuses and sharp words are more common in today's workplace. Forget about looking for warmth; civility is the best we can hope for.

The specific implications of this new environment differ depending on the type of dialogue. The finite nature of jobs, for example, will have a different effect on a conversation in which you're asking an employee to take on more responsibilities than it would on a dialogue in which you're turning down a request for a budget increase. In the former it could provide you with subtle leverage, while in the latter it could suggest a warning that you may not wish to send.

These general and specific changes are what led to the book you now have in your hands. *Workscripts: Perfect Phrases for High-Stakes Conversations* is an entirely new and updated look at the most problematic workplace dialogues, using my successful *Lifescripts* approach as its model. Each of the conversations is treated in a flow-chart form. In this way it's easy to see not only how to start conversations, but how to deal with the most likely responses and how to counter the most likely arguments. Each workscript will have its own introduction to offer guidance on the specific scenario, such as how to approach the conversation, the best days of the week or times of day to have the dialogue, the best locations for the discussion, how to dress and act to improve your chances of success, and what, if any, preparations you should make before the meeting.

Rather than organizing the workscripts based on whom you're speaking with, as I did in earlier books, I've now grouped similar conversations together into chapters. I've done this so that I can get into the specifics about how the new environment affects each type of dialogue. Each of these chapters will begin with a discussion of the new rules for being successful at this type of conversation, in this new workplace world, before examining the individual dialogues. When appropriate, dialogues will be examined from both sides. In other words, I'll explain how to respond to requests for raises from those who work for you, and then how to ask your boss for a raise of your own. In prior editions of *Lifescripts* I went though multiple rounds of back-and-forths in each situation. I've since learned that what readers find most helpful are the first-level responses, and so I've concentrated on those rather than trying to script each possible permutation of a dialogue.

I think it is only appropriate, at such a mercurial time in the workplace, for us to begin with a chapter that focuses on transitions.

Chapter 2

WORKPLACE BOMBSHELLS

With the workplace more unpredictable and chaotic than ever before, I believe there are no more important workplace conversations to master than those dealing with dramatic transitions, the announcements that explode like bombshells in the office.

You might think that in a time when terminations are so common, scripts dealing with those difficult conversations should take priority. While they do of necessity figure prominently in this book, I don't think they're the most important for one simple reason: they almost always represent a fait accompli—an irreversible action. As you'll read when I do cover these scenarios, there's no point trying to argue once a termination agreement has been reached. Energy should instead be directed toward mitigating the impact.

Workplace bombshells are so important because they represent the opposite of a foregone conclusion. The situation is in flux, nothing is established, so you have as much opportunity as you ever will in today's workplace to influence eventual outcomes. Sure, a new boss may already have a personnel plan in place, but since it hasn't yet been enacted you can give them reason to change it. Similarly, employees may have preconceived notions about what a new boss, a relocation, or a reorganization means for their futures, but you still have a chance to affect their reactions.

Whatever transition conversation you're facing, and whatever side you're on in the dialogue, it's important you take into account how the new workplace environment effects these situations.

First, personal rapport is much less important now than it was in previous years.

Experts, myself included, used to suggest that it was important to forge some kind of personal bond with your opposite numbers, not only to make transitional periods smoother, but also to form a warm human connection that could serve as the foundation of future relations. The hope was that managers would give more of a break to employees with whom they had warm relations, or that such a friendship could at least be used as leverage. Also, the thought was that if a new manager was perceived as kind and caring, it would minimize the number of employees who would reflexively jump ship.

Today, no degree of personal affinity makes any difference in managerial decisions; it's all about the money. And with the job market in such a poor state there's little fear of many people jumping ship. Instead, you may have to force people to walk the plank. Now, rather than personal rapport, it's professionalism that matters most. The model for these scenarios isn't people on a blind date, it's members of the military meeting to issue orders and give reports.

Second, spinning and effusiveness won't work. In fact, they're apt to backfire today.

Painting an optimistic picture of a situation—focusing on the glass being half-filled rather than half-empty—has long been a favored management tool for maintaining morale. And when employees still had some trust in management's pronouncements, and hoped for the best in every situation, spin could work. Employee effusiveness could be just as effective a device in years past. Managers always wanted to believe they had the support and goodwill and even admiration of their employees. When workers gushed about how much they loved the company and their jobs, managers tended to believe it and take it as a sign of their own effectiveness as bosses.

Today, spin actually decreases rather than increases discomfort during transitions. Employees are acutely attuned to the reality of their situations. What used to be characterized as a pessimistic attitude can now be viewed only as realism. Managers trying to gloss over reality will be viewed as outright liars, not merely as Pollyannas. Paint a glass as being half-full and employees will think it is almost completely empty. Employees who show excessive emotional commitment to either the company or their boss will be viewed not as enthusiastic supporters but as brown-nosing toadies, dishonest individuals not deserving of rudimentary respect. Effusiveness is likely to hurt rather than help your employment status. The best approaches today are simply to be honest and polite.

Finally, group discussions can now be more effective than one-on-one meetings.

For years it has been thought that meeting face to face with individuals, one at a time, was the best way for a manager to communicate with employees. It was thought to show respect, allow a greater degree of back and forth, and provide better outcomes to dialogues.

But now, the level of fear among employees is so high, and their trust in management is so low, that being singled out in any way at all is instantly perceived as being negative. Being called in to speak to the boss can only be bad. The best way to handle many transition conversations today is to hold them in a group setting. Being one of many gives some employees at least a minimal sense of security in a very insecure environment. And knowing that you are not being singled out in any way protects employee esteem and preserves whatever morale remains.

When the situation is reversed and you're one of the group with whom a transition is being discussed, resist the urge to speak out either to raise an objection, voice a concern, or even ask a question. Nothing good can come of you standing out in this kind of group situation. You'll only mark yourself as a troublemaker or potential problem. If you have an issue that you must address, do it later at a private meeting that you initiate.

To sum up, when dealing with transition conversations today, strive for maximum professionalism, be direct and honest, be polite rather than effusive, and hold group discussions rather than one-on-one conversations whenever possible.

Meeting the New Boss

Your goal when meeting a new boss is to clearly demonstrate you're not a problem. You're a good soldier with a sense of urgency. You're smart, but not so smart as to possibly be construed as a "wise guy" or any kind of threat.

Initiate the meeting by setting up an appointment either directly with the new boss or through his assistant. If you're asked about the reason for the meeting, say you want to introduce yourself and provide a status report.

Prepare for the meeting by drafting a formal memo reporting on the status of all your projects, your staff, and your budget projections. Using this memo as your outline, prepare a complete oral presentation that covers all the points made in your memo. Then, when you have that presentation down pat, prepare a shorter "elevator" version of the presentation that lasts no more than three minutes.

In most cases you'll be leaving this memo behind after your meeting. But don't present it immediately unless you're told you will have only five minutes or you're meeting with the wrong person. If you are interrupted or cut short during your oral presentation, don't let the memo serve as a substitute. That would give your boss an excuse for not meeting with you again. The idea is that the memo should serve as a reinforcement or amplification of your pitch, not a replacement.

Dress the way you normally do at work, making sure there's nothing disconcerting about your appearance or hygiene. Avoid the temptation to scan the boss's office looking for cues and hints about him or her. Maintain eye contact except to consult your notes.

If you're told you have only a few minutes, launch into your "elevator" pitch and use your memo as a supplemental "leave behind." If you're told there will be a reorganization and you'll actually be reporting to someone else, don't characterize the shift in any way. Instead, explain you'll set up a meeting with your new boss as soon as possible, ask to provide a brief status report, give your "elevator" pitch, and leave your memo behind as a supplement.

If you're ambushed with a problem you're aware of, explain how the issue is an *obstacle* rather than a problem. This is more than a semantic dodge. It demonstrates that the issue is temporary and that a solution has already been found. If you're not aware of the problem, don't deny it. Explain that it's a surprise to you, that you'll investigate it further, and that you will get back as soon as possible.

Close your conversation with a simple thanks for the meeting and a polite, but not excessive, expression of best wishes. See Workscript 2.1.

Workscript 2.1 Meeting your new boss

Icebreaker: Mr. Trump, I'm [your name]. It's good to meet you. I wanted to introduce myself and give you a status report on the projects I'm working on.

An ambush: *I'm glad you're here. I was going to call you in. I hear there's a problem in your department and we're going to take a financial hit.*

Not much time: *It's good to meet you too. I have a very busy schedule and usually set these meetings up on my own. I've only got 5 minutes for you.*

Not me: *I'm glad to meet you, but I'm the wrong person for you to speak with. I'm reorganizing and you'll be reporting to Ms. Stewart.*

Let's hear it: *Great to meet you. I'm glad you set this meeting. Tell me how things are going.*

18

You're surprised: Could you be more specific? I haven't had any indication of a problem. I'll look into it immediately and get back to you.

Not surprised: I assume you're talking about the apprentice project. I wouldn't characterize it as a problem. It's just an obstacle we're in the process of overcoming. [Launch into full report]

Quick pitch: I know you're very busy. I'll be as concise as possible and leave a copy of the full report with you. First, we're not facing any major problems. [Launch into elevator pitch]

Will do, but: I'll set up a meeting with Ms. Stewart right away. What I'd like to do now is just give you a very quick status report and leave a copy of the full report with you. [Launch into elevator pitch]

Planned pitch: First, we're not facing any major problems. [Launch into full pitch]

Meeting Your New Staff

When you meet your direct "reports" for the first time, the most important thing you need to accomplish is to plant the seeds of future teamwork and community. That's true whether you're a complete outsider, or someone coming in from another part of the company, or you've been promoted to now lead your former peers.

An obvious way to signal the importance of teamwork is to make sure your first "meet and greet" is done in a group setting. Avoid preliminary one-on-one meetings if possible, to avoid sending a message that some are "insiders" or more important than others.

This group introduction should take place as early in the week and in the day as practical. That will let you issue marching orders that can be acted on immediately so the team is all pulling together from day one. End-of-week introductions could lead to weekend intrigue, gossip, and fear.

Pay careful attention to your garb. You want to give yourself the appearance of leadership, while not putting too much distance between yourself and the rest of the team. If you're coming in from outside, and are as a result largely uninformed about the staff, wear conservative, formal business attire. That means nothing flashy and no "bling." If you're coming in from another department or have been promoted from the ranks, simply turn your attire up one subtle notch of formality. For example, wear a suit if you usually dress in separates; don a jacket if previously you were always in shirtsleeves. You want everyone to know you're at a higher level, but you don't want to look like you just won the lottery or have forgotten your "roots."

It's essential you avoid spin and propaganda. Don't ignore the hard truths or explain them away. You can expect people to ask questions to which they already know the answers in an effort to test your honesty and directness. Saying there will be no changes is prima facie absurd; your simply being there is a change. These people haven't been living in a bunker for the past few years: they know how business works.

If personnel cuts have been planned prior to your arrival, vehemently push for them to be carried out before you take the helm. If you come in as the grim reaper, the impression will be permanent: You'll never win the existing staff over. You want to be the one who helps pick up the pieces and puts the team back together, rather than the one who tears the group apart.

Acknowledge whatever fears are expressed and demonstrate openness to even the most trivial, small-picture issues that are raised. Explain that the only stupid question is the one that goes unasked. You want everyone to feel that they are being heard and that you'll be open even to their particular, private concerns.

Stress that this is a new day, not only for you but for the whole team. The past is the past. From this moment you are all on the same path with the same goal. See Workscript 2.2.

Explaining a Restructuring

Whether your group has been incorporated into an entirely new division or now reports to a different executive team, the problem is the same: free-floating uncertainty. Today, even in the best of times, there's a constant low-grade uncertainty in the workplace. When a restructuring has been announced, those fears rise to the surface and threaten to dominate the workday. Your goal is to calm everyone, to the greatest extent possible, so that you can get on with business.

Workscript 2.2 Meeting your new staff

Intro and pitch: I want to thank you all for coming. We'll be talking a lot about specifics in the coming days, but this morning there are really only two points I want to make. First, today is a fresh start, not just for me, but for all of us. Second, we all have one shared goal: to boost revenue ten percent this year. Everything we do is directed toward achieving that. I'm sure you have questions, so fire away.

Worried about status: *Are you going to be making any changes in the way the department is organized or in our responsibilities?*

Worried about job: *Are there any staff cuts coming?*

Personal pet peeve: *We've never gotten any support from the sales staff and that's really hurt our results. Will you be able to take care of that and get sales on board?*

Jealous you got the job: *We've all worked together in the past so I was wondering how you think you'll be able to change things?*

22

Nothing is predetermined: Change is almost a given these days, so I'm sure things will be different, but I promise you that I'm not coming in here with any predetermined plans or fixed ideas. We're in this together and I want to speak with all of you to get your ideas.

Nothing is planned: We all know what the workplace is like these days, but I promise you that right now there are no planned personnel changes.

Acknowledgment: This is an important issue and it's just the kind of thing I'll need your help in solving. I promise you that we'll do what we have to do to achieve our goal.

I have insights: My experience working here with all of you gives me insights into our strengths and weaknesses. I have some ideas and I look forward to hearing from everyone here who's interested in reaching our goal.

23

This is another discussion that should be held as a group. The specific day of the week and time of day matters less than that you have the meeting as soon as possible after the restructuring becomes common knowledge. If the word leaks out and the gossip starts, you may not even be able to wait for an official announcement. You want to calm your staff at the first sign of agitation.

The best way to do this is to be the ultimate source of rationality. Keep the issue in perspective. Report the facts honestly while reining in those who are jumping to conclusions. Explain that a restructuring is almost always done for organizational reasons and has nothing to do with personnel matters. That doesn't preclude future cutbacks, it just means the issues are separate.

Stress that you are all part of a team, and that you will still all be working together toward the same goals you'd had before the reorganization. Having everyone together, being honest and rational, and stressing continuity will mitigate fears and uncertainty. See Workscript 2.3.

Announcing a Purchase or Merger

Other than imminent mass firings, or impending bankruptcy, the most stressful news employees can receive is that their employer has been purchased or is merging with another company.

Besides the normal fear of change, mergers or purchases by existing organizations carry with them the specter of wholesale changes. It's assumed, correctly, that widespread staff cuts often follow such a purchase. After all, one of the ways companies justify purchases is by calculating the economies of scale that could result. One combined sales team, for instance, is cheaper than two independent teams.

Even if the purchase is entrepreneurial, and represents only new management, changes are likely on the way. It's the rare individual who buys a new business and isn't tempted to put his or her mark on the company. That could mean something as benign as cosmetic change or as profound as a new approach to finances.

Ignoring or denying that changes, including possible staff or budget cuts, are likely, won't comfort your staff. It will only tar you as a dissembler, making them feel worse since now they'll feel like they're being led over the cliff by a liar.

What's needed is for you to frame what has happened as a generally positive sign. After all, a purchase or merger is a sign that the buyer values what is being bought. While short-term changes are likely, being valued by the new ownership means there's a long-term future for the organization.

This is another problematic discussion mitigated somewhat by a group setting. The more fears and concerns aired in this kind of controlled environment, the fewer whispered conversations will be held around the coffee pot.

If possible, hold this meeting after lunch, early in the week. Hold it in the morning and no work will get done the rest of the day. Hold it at the end of the week and imaginations will run wild over the weekend. Set aside as much time as necessary to answer any and all questions. Your goal is to provide accurate information in a realistic perspective to calm fears and minimize the time spent on the matter. See Workscript 2.4.

Announcing a Relocation

The most difficult business relocations are those that offer an employee no way to keep his or her job unless major life change is undertaken, such as moving to a new home and the uprooting of a spouse and/or school-age children that results.

Workscript 2.3 Explaining a restructuring

It's all about bureaucracy: I'm sure you've all heard the rumors about the reorganization. The company has decided that from now on we will report to the marketing department rather than the sales department. This isn't a judgment on our performance or value. It's based solely on their judgment that this will be more profitable for the company.

Worried about job: *Will we all still be staying together?*

Who's this guy? *What can you tell us about our new vice president?*

Worried about future: *Does this reflect a change in the company's philosophy?*

What will they think? *How do I explain this to my customers?*

But what about us? *How will this effect how we do our jobs?*

26

Not the issue: *Internal personnel issues aren't part of this restructuring; they are a completely separate issue. This is only about the table of organization.*

She's okay: *This is going to be a learning process for all of us. I know that she's smart, objective, and open to learning what we do and how we do it. That's everything we could ask for.*

About the money: *Not at all. The company's priority is, and will remain, to be as profitable as possible. This is just one more step to reaching that goal.*

Don't worry: *The company will be sending out a release on the change, but you can assure your customers that they'll receive the same great service they've had before.*

It won't: *This isn't about what we do inside this office; it's about how we fit into the rest of the company. We're going to keep doing what we have been doing.*

27

Workscript 2.4 Announcing a purchase or merger

Break the news: I wanted to let you all know that the rumors are true. The company has been sold. We've been purchased by Jane Smith, an entrepreneur who has been looking for a business like ours. [or] We've been purchased by Alpha, Inc., owner of a number of other companies similar to our own. I don't have details on any planned changes, but I think we can safely assume there will be some. However, what's important to remember is that our company has been purchased because the new owner believes we are valuable now and can become even more valuable. That means this purchase creates opportunities for all of us. Questions?

Do they know what they're doing? *Are they familiar with our business?*

Are we safe? *Are they planning to cut staff?*

Will they interfere? *How will this effect the way we do business?*

Benefits safe? *How will this effect our benefits package and retirement plans? I've heard their plan isn't as good as ours.*

28

→ **Good either way:** Yes, and that's a good thing. It means they know we're good at what we do. [or] I don't believe so, but that's a good thing because they have no preconceived notions and we can teach them about what we do.

→ **No promises:** I wouldn't be surprised if there are people left behind. That's just the reality of business today. The good news for those of us who remain is that we'll be part of a healthier company which provides real future opportunities.

→ **Only get better:** There's always room for improvement. I'm sure they'll have ideas and input, but remember, they are buying us because they like what we've done in the past and think we can do even better in the future.

→ **Focus on what matters:** Ultimately I'm sure all our packages will be replaced. I don't know whether that will be for the better or worse. What I do know is that it's better to have a job with an organization that is healthy than to lose a job that had wonderful benefits.

Workscript 2.5 Announcing a relocation

We're moving: The company has decided to relocate to Northbrook, Illinois, a suburb of Chicago. We want all of you to make the move with us. We know this is potentially traumatic, so we have hired a consulting firm to help with the sale and purchase or rental of real estate and the shifting of schools, as well as other transition issues. We're announcing this on a Friday to give you time to speak with your families. We'll be expecting your decision about whether you'll be relocating with us in six weeks. If anyone decides not to relocate they will receive the same severance package as if they were fired without cause. I'm here to answer any questions you have and the consultants will be here next week to provide even more detail on their services. Questions?

Bad time to sell: *The real estate market is down right now so we could lose money on the sale of our homes.*

Rental help: From what I understand the company will provide temporary rental assistance so people don't have to sell their homes under time pressure and take a big loss. The consultants will be able to provide more details on the program.

Job protection? *What kind of job protection can we expect if we make the move. After all, no one wants to relocate and then find themselves out of work.*

Re-relocation: We can't make any guarantees, however the company will provide the same assistance in re-relocating, as well as a full severance package, to anyone who makes the move and who is fired within 12 months of making the move.

Time off? *When will we have the time to look for new places to live and new schools?*

Travel time and money: Part of the package will include time off as well as paid transportation for a preliminary trip for everyone who will be making the move.

Not fair: *You know you're really shaking up our lives. This is almost like firing us.*

Your choice: We know how traumatic this is and we're going to do our best to ease the process. We want you all to come, but if this is simply too traumatic for you then you can choose not to come with us and instead take the severance package.

Cost of living? *Isn't the cost of living much higher there than here? Will we be getting cost of living increases?*

→ **No increase:** There's no plan for an across-the-board cost of living increase. The choice isn't between having your current income in your current location and your current income in a new location. It's a choice between having your current income in a new location and having no income in your current location.

Clients? *What do we tell our clients and customers when they ask why we're moving?*

→ **Nothing:** The company will be issuing a press release and contacting clients directly so you don't have to tell them yourself. If they ask, you can just reassure them they'll be receiving the same great service [or] products they are now.

Special need? *My mother is in a nursing home and I'm her only relative. Will the company help relocate her?*

→ **We'll talk:** We know that some of you may have special needs. We and the relocation consultants will be happy to speak with anyone about specific issues they may have.

Telecommute? *Is the company open to some of us telecommuting rather than relocating? Maybe we could do our jobs via the Internet.*

→ **Not an option:** We explored that idea before deciding on the relocation. We decided it simply wasn't a viable option and so we won't be offering that as an alternative to relocating.

31

Typically, these relocations are done because a new owner or executive team demands it, or company strategists decide that a new location will provide a business advantage. The news is usually broken to the rank-and-file only after upper management has signed onto the move. It's vital that you stress that the company wants everyone to come along and sees them all as part of its future.

Losing the majority of existing staff and having to rehire new employees in a new location represents an extraordinary expense and disruption to operations. As a result, companies will provide considerable support, financial and otherwise, to help employees through the move. Help in the sale and purchase of real estate and in registering children in new schools are standard elements in these packages. Employees who choose not to relocate are almost always offered the same severance package they'd receive if they were fired without cause. Employees need to be given as much time as possible to decide if they want to make the move. Six weeks should be the minimum time period. Do your best to have the details of the entire support package before you announce the relocation.

It's vital that the announcement be made to everyone at the same time so there's no hint of favoritism. No one is going to be happy about this, but you want to minimize, to the greatest extent possible, all the inevitable gossiping and complaining. Do this after lunch on a Friday. That way you'll minimize the amount of work time devoted to griping while providing them with an immediate opportunity to discuss the matter with their family. This is, primarily, a personal decision. And as a result, it should be something they can immediately discuss with the family.

Stress your openness to fielding any question and in your responses make clear your honesty and openness. This is no time for spin or obfuscation. Be direct, honest, and rational. Make your case, lay out the facts, and let your employees decide for themselves. Don't try to minimize the impact of the relocation. Simply stress the opportunity it provides and lay out the details of the support the company is offering.

Your goal in this presentation is to minimize the reflexive anger over the move, stress the opportunities the shift offers, and provide all the details you can so your employees make an informed decision. See Workscript 2.5.

Chapter 3

DEATH SENTENCES

One thing that's certainly different in today's workplace is that terminations have become more frequent than in the past. Managers used to be able to go for years without having to deliver a death sentence. Terminating an employee used to be considered a milestone for a young manager, a big step in the process of professional maturation, made even larger because it was so rare. While it's still monumental and traumatic for the employee being fired, it's no longer as significant an event for the manager. That's a shame.

Primarily, it's a shame because it makes management a less humane process. Terminations are a fact of business. Based, in one way or another, on economic factors, they are neither good nor evil; they're just facts. But when they were rare, and still meaningful, events for management as well as for employees, they were handled with far more sensitivity and compassion. In years past no one would have thought to not let someone clean up his or her own desk or to have a long-time employee escorted out and away from the building by a security guard as if they were a criminal. Treating someone with dignity and respect was important, not because it yielded some tangible return, but because it was the right thing to do and it sent a message to everyone else in the organization. Today there is no compassion, sensitivity, or empathy in the termination process.

It's also a process that has been changed in substance, not just tone, by the new work environment. The rarity of face-to-face communications now means that the moment you ask anyone to come into your office they will assume they are being fired. This means there's no longer as much pressure in "breaking the news" the right way. You have, in effect, broken the news when you ask, "Could you please come in to my office?"

Because short-term performance is all that matters in today's workplace, prior successes and previous excellent performance are now no longer defenses against termination. Someone can be the company's top performer for two years running and a single down quarter can result in being let go. This can eliminate the need to build up a paper trail of negative performance reviews to justify termination. A manager today needn't worry that just six months earlier he or she gave a positive review to an employee who's now being fired.

Similarly, the realization that all jobs now have expiration dates means that even someone who's performing well in the short term can be let go, not just with impunity, but also with little need for explanation. If the role an individual plays for a company is no longer necessary, they are expendable.

These are some of the reasons why there's no trust in today's workplace. The relationship between management and employees is now toxic. This means that you must expect that nothing you say or promise will be believed unless it is put in writing. Whatever severance package is being provided must now be thoroughly documented.

Because today's workplace environment makes terminating an employee so much easier, I believe you should do everything in your power to make the execution process as humane as you can, without jeopardizing your own employment. At a time when rationalizations and reasons for terminations are almost unnecessary, and when employees are so mistrustful that they come to work almost expecting the axe to fall, it's important to act as compassionately as possible. Not for any business reason, but for a personal one: it's the right thing to do. Even in the Middle Ages, when people were often killed unjustly, the executioner did his best to make a clean, swift kill out of professional pride and mercy. A twenty-first-century manager today should at least have the scruples of a thirteenth-century executioner. To the extent possible, treat people the way you would want to be treated.

As you'll see in this chapter the typical termination meeting has become so common and legalistic that it is done according to a formal script. Despite this standardization there are still some termination scenarios that, even in today's environment, remain problematic. It's important to note that all of these dialogues involve individual, rather than mass firings. The former allow for the kind of flexibility spelled out in the pages that follow. The latter must be done strictly by the book to ensure total equity of pain and suffering and therefore minimize the company's legal liability.

Of course, it's even more problematic if you're the one being terminated. While situation specific rejoinders are offered in the rest of this chapter, there are some general rules you should keep in mind.

First, banish from your mind all thoughts of reinstatement. Groucho Marx once joked that he'd never want to join any club that would accept him as a member. Well, you never want to work for any company that would consider firing you. Besides, in the more than 40 years I've been advising clients

I've seen only a handful of reinstatements, and every one of those resulted in a subsequent termination, often in less time than the severance would have lasted.

That leads to the second rule: it's all about the money. While severance may not be a legal obligation, it is such an accepted practice that no employer today can fire someone without cause, not pay severance, and expect to be able to successfully retain or recruit employees. And not only is severance a de facto rule, it's also completely negotiable. In mass firings companies will offer and stand by standardized packages. But in individual firings companies have, and build in, flexibility. The severance offer you're presented with is the lowest number in a range, so ask for more.

Third, understand there's more to the money than severance pay. Anything that would cost you money out of pocket is something you can ask your former employer to pay for as part of your separation package. COBRA payments, outplacement counseling, training, secretarial help, and anything else you can think of can be part of your counteroffer.

There's no reason to rein in requests if you've been terminated. After all, what else can they do to you? They've already done their worst.

The Termination of a Company Icon

While terminating an employee has never been easier, there's one type of termination that remains extraordinarily difficult, requiring a great deal of preparation and thought: the firing of a company icon.

A company icon is someone known by everyone in the organization and industry. He or she is strongly associated with the company, perhaps is even the personification of the organization in people's eyes. The termination of a company icon will have an impact both inside and outside the organization. Other employees will have their feelings of vulnerability reinforced and magnified: "If they could fire him, no one is ever safe." Morale is likely to take a hit and anger at and distrust of the organization will rise. Customers, vendors, suppliers, and industry observers will question the decision-making and health of the company. Those questions will likely be echoed by competitors, who will actively encourage speculation: "Did you hear they actually fired her?"

Your goals in this dialogue are to minimize the impact on internal morale and mitigate the damage to the company's external image. The best way to accomplish those two objectives is to make the soon-to-be former company icon a partner in his or her own termination. That's done by trying to provide as dignified an exit as possible.

While it's usually best to terminate employees on a Monday so they can immediately launch their recovery efforts, terminating a company icon should take place on Friday, after lunch. You don't want the rest of the organization spending the remaining workweek gossiping about what happened. You also don't want the former icon to have to walk the gauntlet of former coworkers on his or her way out the building.

It has become standard practice in many firms for human resources (HR) to send a representative to sit in on termination meetings. The idea is to create an impersonal, formal tone, deter outbursts, and to provide expertise in technical matters. In the case of a company icon, however, it would only serve to exacerbate the employee's sense of betrayal and embarrassment: After being the personal embodiment of the firm, she is now being treated impersonally. By all means consult with them beforehand, but unless you expect some kind of emotional problem you should fight to keep HR out of this meeting. In addition, do all that you can to keep security from getting actively involved. If you're told that in this scenario "everyone" is kept out of his or her office and "everyone" is escorted from the building, simply note that this employee isn't "everyone." Special people deserve special treatment.

The only reason for firing an icon that cannot be countered is that his or her job simply no longer exists. This rationale has the added benefit of being no reflection on the employee's performance. And no one outside the organization could really quarrel with letting someone go whose job is extinct, no matter how loyally and well they've served.

In addition to whatever severance package is being offered, provide the icon with the opportunity to jointly frame how their departure will be characterized. You want to be able to release a statement from the perspectives of both the company and the former icon that explains what has transpired. Explain that, moving forward, it will be of enormous benefit to both parties for this to be seen as an amicable parting. If the employee wants to call this a resignation to pursue other opportunities, or an early retirement to address personal needs and wants, that's fine. His or her partnership in the process is so valuable that it's worth buying it with an expanded severance package if necessary. See Workscript 3.1.

If you're the company icon being terminated, you need to use your legal leverage to get as much as you possibly can out of your former employer. There are state and federal statutes that prevent employers from discriminating based on age or seniority. And while, if they're savvy, they've probably done the minimum they need to protect themselves, that doesn't mean you're powerless. Just the threat of legal action with even a minimal chance of success is enough to make most employers blink. Employers know there are plaintiff's attorneys out there willing to take on wrongful termination suits for contingency fees, so employees won't need to pay out-of-pocket. They, on the other hand, will be liable for legal fees and will also suffer public scorn.

Besides asking for a larger severance package, look to change the terms of any termination agreement. Most such agreements have restrictive covenants that look to bar you from doing certain activities in exchange for the severance. Work to weaken these. Many of these agreements also make severance payouts conditional, which means that they cease if you obtain another job before they otherwise would have run out. Insist that your severance, as a former company icon, cannot be mitigated. Justify the request by noting that their action will create a mountain of debt for you.

Finally, if you don't get satisfaction in this conversation, don't give up. There's no reason that a company icon like yourself can't demand a face-to-face with someone higher up. Ironically, the higher up you go, the more you're likely to get. See Workscript 3.2.

Friends Firing Friends

No matter how often we're advised to keep our personal and business lives separate, they invariably become intertwined the longer we hold a particular position. That's only natural, since we spend most of our waking hours in the workplace. But there are times when the connections lead to problems. With all the terminations taking place, it's now likely every manager will one day be required to fire a close friend.

It's your duty as a friend to do everything you possibly can, short of risking your own employment, to forestall this termination. You need to do whatever you'd expect a friend to do to protect you if the situation were reversed. Unfortunately, even these extensive efforts may not be enough. Faced with no chance of saving your friend's job, your goals must be to minimize his or her discomfort and to maintain the friendship.

Approach this as a two-stage conversation, mirroring the two types of relationships you have with this individual. You

Workscript 3.1 Terminating a company icon

Job no longer exists: You know as much about this company and the industry as anyone, so I don't think you'll be surprised when I tell you that the company is eliminating your position. Your job simply has become extinct. We'll be providing you with a severance package appropriate for someone of your tenure. [Explain package] We'd also like to give you the opportunity to coauthor the announcement of your departure so you can frame it in a manner that would be of the most benefit for you, going ahead.

I'll need more: *You're right that it's not a surprise. But it's still a disappointment. I think I'd like to say that I'm leaving to pursue my own business . . . but that's going to be an expensive undertaking. Another year's severance would be very helpful.*

Another chance: *I've been here for so long. Isn't there something else I could do for the company? I'd be happy to shift to another job even if it's not as prestigious as the one I have now. If you give me another six months maybe things will change.*

Don't you know who I am? *You can't do this to me. I've been the face of this company for 20 years. If anyone should be fired it's Johnson. I've given this company everything and this is how I'm repaid? I want to talk to Mr. King and have him tell me this to my face.*

42

→ **Negotiate:** I don't think that would be a problem. [or] While I don't think we can provide another year's severance, we can pick up the cost of COBRA for another year and provide you with use of your office for six months. Now let's talk about the announcement.

→ **No hope:** We've already explored all the options and this decision is final. One place we do have flexibility is in how your departure is portrayed to your peers and the outside world. Together we can together craft an announcement that puts you in the best light, moving forward.

→ **Anger won't help:** I understand your anger but it won't change the situation. Mr. King knows about your leaving; he asked me to handle it. We're well aware of all you've meant to the company. That's why we're giving you the severance package I outlined and we're giving you the chance to frame your departure the way you'd like.

Workscript 3.2 You're the icon being terminated

Job no longer exists: *You know as much about this company and the industry as anyone, so I don't think you'll be surprised when I tell you that the company is eliminating your position. Your job simply has become extinct. We'll be providing you with a severance package appropriate for someone of your tenure. [Explains package] We'd also like to give you the opportunity to coauthor the announcement of your departure so you can frame it in a manner that would be of the most benefit for your going ahead.*

→

I am surprised: *Actually I am surprised because I thought the government would protect me. I don't know how much my age factored into this decision, but I need you to realize that by doing this you're not just terminating my job, but my entire career. At my age I would need retraining in an entirely different field. I will never be able to get another job paying anywhere near what I'm currently earning. Your severance package isn't going to bridge me to another job in any meaningful way. I'll need you to provide me with [provide details of what you want in your package].*

→

If you don't receive an acceptable response, turn to Workscript 3.11, Making an end run around your boss, on page 66.

44

will have a traditional, formal manager/employee termination meeting at the appointed time. However you should precede that dialogue with an informal friend-to-friend discussion.

This informal meeting should take place outside the workplace. Having it over coffee, drinks, or a meal at a place where you'll be able to have a confidential talk is best. Hold it as soon as you realize the termination is inevitable.

After explaining the situation realistically, you need to demonstrate, through words and deeds, that you will continue to help your friend as much as possible. You can do that by encouraging your friend to become involved in the process rather than sitting back and meekly accepting what is offered. You might even subtly suggest areas of the severance package that might be open to further negotiation. See Workscript 3.3.

If your good friend has just told you that he or she has to fire you, you have to take advantage of their guilt and inevitable offers of personal help. For the moment, don't look at this person as your friend; look at them as a tool you can wield to mitigate the effects of what is happening. Instead of asking for personal help, prod them for as much information as possible about the severance package you'll be offered and how much flexibility they've been given. Having just told you they'll be firing you, and having offered whatever personal help they can provide, they aren't going to be able to withhold any information. Your goal is to get inside information to help in your preparation of a counteroffer, and to smooth the way for going over your friend's head if necessary. See Workscript 3.4.

Terminating SomeoJne Close to Retirement

When you're forced to fire someone who is one year from being fully vested in a retirement plan, you need to tread very carefully. If instead of terminating them, you can find another position in the company for the person, even if it's at a lower salary and only for a year, it's worth the effort.

Workscript 3.3 Firing a friend

Break the news: I've got bad news for you. I got word yesterday that I have to fire you. I've done everything I could to prevent this, but it's inevitable. I wanted to give you advance warning and see if there was anything I could do to help and to let you know that I'll be here for you as your friend to help in any way I can.

Any hope: *Isn't there anything I can do to forestall this, or delay it? What about going to talk to Ms. Big and offering to take a pay cut?*

Gets angry: *Couldn't you have let me know sooner? Couldn't you have kept me off the list?*

Personal trouble: *Debbie's tuition bill comes due in a couple of months. What am I going to do?*

No future: *What am I going to do now? No one is going to hire someone my age.*

46

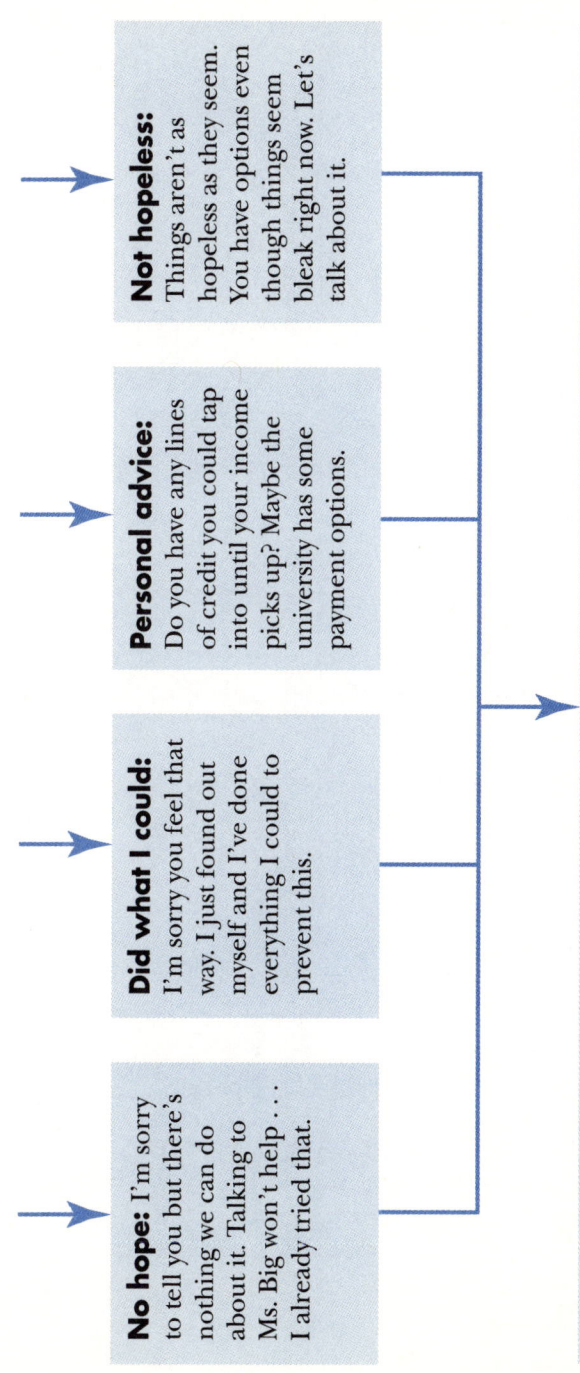

No hope: I'm sorry to tell you but there's nothing we can do about it. Talking to Ms. Big won't help . . . I already tried that.

Did what I could: I'm sorry you feel that way. I just found out myself and I've done everything I could to prevent this.

Personal advice: Do you have any lines of credit you could tap into until your income picks up? Maybe the university has some payment options.

Not hopeless: Things aren't as hopeless as they seem. You have options even though things seem bleak right now. Let's talk about it.

Take charge: Meanwhile, the first thing you can do is realize you've got some power in the process. For example, I think that there's room in the severance package for some negotiation. If you came back and asked for outplacement counseling, or an extension of the COBRA coverage, I think you might find there's some flexibility.

47

Workscript 3.4 Being fired by a friend

Break the news: *I've got bad news for you. I got word yesterday that I have to fire you. I've done everything I could to prevent this but it's inevitable. I wanted to give you advance warning and see if there was anything I could do to help and to let you know that I'll be here for you as your friend to help in any way I can.*

What can I get? *Thanks for giving me the heads-up. I really appreciate it. You know that the standard severance package the company offers won't work for me; it won't be enough to bridge me to another job, especially with all the personal issues I'm facing. I don't know how much you can personally expand the package and in what areas. Should I just go directly to see Ms. Big, or will you be able to provide me with, say, [mention desired expanded package]?*

If that's not possible and your organization has an HR department, this is one instance when it's worth having a personnel expert sit in on the meeting. Sure, it may make the meeting feel more formal, but it's apt to minimize legal exposure. Before the meeting takes place, advocate for the firm giving the employee credit for the remaining year so they become fully vested. Providing this "bridging" as part of a severance package will remove the issue that makes this firing more problematic than a typical termination.

If you can't obtain the added year's credit for the employee, you'll be forced to resort to the typical, highly formalized, cold termination script. In that case, do the job as quickly as possible and take whatever solace you can in the fact that you tried your best to help. See Workscript 3.5.

If you're terminated when close to retirement, you have two possible responses, based on whether or not your former employer has done the right thing and "bridged" your seniority to the vesting level. Don't let the company's gesture suffice. Ask that, in the same spirit, the company also carry the cost of your health coverage until it's covered by your retirement or pension plan. Having already established the bridging precedent, it's not much of a leap for the company to broaden it to include health coverage. If the company hasn't given you credit for whatever time you need to earn your retirement benefits, don't hesitate to use your legal leverage. The specter of a wrongful termination suit should be sufficient to increase your severance package . . . and that's what it's all about. See Workscript 3.6.

Terminating Someone with a Personal Burden

Firing someone with a personal burden, such as a disabled or sick dependent, may not be as fraught with legal issues as firing someone close to retirement, but it's weightier on an emotional level.

Workscript 3.5 Terminating someone close to retirement

Opener: Your employment here is being terminated. This decision was based on the company's economic health. The decision was made at the highest levels and is final.

Able to get credit: We're aware that you are one year away from being fully vested in the retirement plan and, as part of your severance package, have arranged for you to receive one year's credit so that after signing this acceptance letter you will be fully vested.

Unable to get credit: The company has prepared a severance package for you. I have a check already cut which I can provide you after you've signed this acceptance letter.

Appreciative: *I appreciate that. Isn't there anything I can do to keep my job?*

Age issue: *You've singled me out because of my age and my being one year away from being fully vested.*

Do something: *I've worked here for almost 20 years. I'm one year away from being vested. Isn't there something you can do for me?*

50

No hope: There's nothing I can do. We're appreciative of your service. That's why we've put together this severance package.

Not a factor: Neither your age nor seniority were factors in this decision. It was based on the company's current economic needs. If you sign this, I'll be able to give you a check for your severance.

Resists: *I'm not going to sign anything until I've had a chance to speak with my attorney.*

Ok: You have every right to speak with a lawyer. I'll hold onto the check until I hear from you.

No hope: There's nothing I can do. If you sign this I'll be able to give you a severance check and have an updated pension statement sent to you.

Workscript 3.6 Being terminated when close to retirement

Opener: *Your employment here is being terminated. This decision was based on the company's economic health. The decision was made at the highest levels and is final.*

Able to get credit: *We're aware that you are one year away from being fully vested in the retirement plan and, as part of your severance package, have arranged for you to receive one year's credit so that after signing this acceptance letter you will be fully vested.*

Unable to get credit: *The company has prepared a severance package for you. I have a check already cut which I can provide you after you've signed this acceptance letter.*

Ask for more: I appreciate that. You obviously know that because of my age it's unlikely I'll be able to find another position that offers the kind of health coverage I'm receiving now. In addition to bridging me to retirement, I'd like the company to pick up the cost of COBRA coverage until my retirement medical coverage becomes effective.

Not good enough: I don't know how much my proximity to retirement age factored into this decision, but I need you to realize that by doing this you're not just terminating my job but my entire career. At my age I would need retraining in an entirely different field. I will never be able to get another job paying anywhere near what I'm currently earning and I'll never be able to build up the retirement benefits I've accrued here. Your severance offer isn't sufficient. I'll need you to bridge my seniority so I become vested in the retirement plan and also provide me with . . . [provide details of what you want in your package].

If you don't receive an acceptable response, turn to Workscript 3.11, Making an end run around your boss, on page 66.

53

Try to keep HR out of this meeting in order to set a more personal, caring tone. Once again, do some preliminary investigation to see what the company can do for the employee in terms of contributing to the cost of ongoing medical coverage. Let the employee know that you are aware of their special burden and have tried to do whatever you could to help. Successful or not, your effort may dilute some of their anger.

Without HR there, you'll be freer to sympathize with their situation. However don't say you know how they feel, unless you actually share the same burden and have found yourself in the same situation. False empathy may spark rather than dampen anger.

As with other difficult, but unavoidable, terminations, do your best, do it quickly, and try to put it behind you. See Workscript 3.7.

If 'you or a dependent have a special personal need and you find yourself being terminated, it's important to channel your anger and fear. Your goal is to do everything you possibly can to provide for you or your dependent's needs. That may mean seeming ungrateful or appearing vengeful. If the company makes some gesture in acknowledgement of your situation, such as offering to pick up the cost of COBRA, don't hesitate to say it's insufficient and ask for more. And if the company offers nothing other than sympathy, I'd suggest threatening legal action.

Understand that it's unlikely you actually have any legal leverage in this case. However, the threat of being sued by a vengeful aggrieved former employee with a very sympathetic story to tell should be enough to extract a better severance package. Ironically, the less actual legal leverage you have, the more aggressive you need to be in threatening action. See Workscript 3.8.

Terminating Someone . . . But Asking Them to Remain Available

There are times when an employee being terminated has special knowledge or contacts the company would like to retain during a transitional period. Perhaps the former employee can provide unique insights into the attitudes and behavior of key customers. Or maybe he or she is the only one who understands a novel filing or information system that is in the process of being made more universally accessible.

No terminated employee will be eager to help out the company that has just let him or her go. The only way to get this kind of cooperation or continued availability will be to pay for it, in one form or another. Begin by offering to frame the departure as a resignation rather than a termination, and announcing that the former employee's continued presence is at the company's request.

The quid pro quo arrangement can include some combination of a generous severance package, continued use of office facilities, a short-term consulting arrangement, or even continued benefits for the duration of the arrangement. The extent of the deal will depend on how much the company can afford and the value of the expertise of the former employee.

The arrangement can terminate early if the former employee gets another position, or be extended if mutually agreed after the initial time period expires. See Workscript 3.9.

If you're terminated, but asked to remain available for a transitional period, you could try to negotiate the best "consulting" package, but consider taking matters a step further.

It is always easier to get a job when you're still employed. Even in the most difficult of economic times, companies harbor at least an element of doubt about anyone who is

Workscript 3.7 Terminating someone with a personal burden

Opener: Your employment here is being terminated. This decision was based on the company's economic health. The decision was made at the highest levels and is final.

Able to get help: I'm aware that you have some special family needs. In addition to the normal severance package for someone of your tenure, we've arranged to pick up the cost of your COBRA for six months or until you receive other coverage.

Unable to get credit: I'm aware that you have some special family needs and did my best to get you the most severance I could. I have a check already cut which I can provide you after you've signed this termination letter.

Appreciative: *I appreciate that. Isn't there anything I can do to keep my job?*

↓

No hope: There's nothing I can do. If you sign this termination letter I'll be able to give you a severance check and get the COBRA payments started.

Do something: *I've got a family member with considerable medical needs. Isn't there something you can do for me?*

Upset: *I appreciate your efforts, but I don't think the company realizes what this will mean for my family. I don't know what I'm going to do.*

No hope: I know your situation and sympathize. I will be of whatever personal help I can, but there's nothing more the company can do. If you sign this letter I can provide you with the severance check.

Half-hearted defense: The company's position is that it couldn't make special arrangements for any one individual. I will do whatever I can personally to help, but all I can do now is ask you to sign this letter.

57

Workscript 3.8 Being terminated when you have a personal burden

Opener: *Your employment here is being terminated. This decision was based on the company's economic health. The decision was made at the highest levels and is final.*

Able to get help: *I'm aware that you have some special family needs. In addition to the normal severance package for someone of your tenure, we've arranged to pick up the cost of your COBRA for six months or until you receive other coverage.*

Unable to get credit: *I'm aware that you have some special family needs and did my best to get you the most severance I could. I have a check already cut which I can provide you after you've signed this termination letter.*

Appreciative, but: I appreciate that. But what you're providing me with really is just interim help. We both know what the job market is like and that six months will probably not be sufficient time for me to find another job that provides health coverage for my family. What I need from the company is more financial help so that my family can survive this termination.

Lawyer up: Who should I tell my lawyer to speak with about this? I don't know whether I'm being unfairly singled out because of my family's medical issues., but I do know that this is going to create an extraordinarily difficult situation for my family which this severance package does little to mitigate.

If you don't receive an acceptable response, turn to Workscript 3.11, Making an end run around your boss, on page 66.

Workscript 3.9 Terminating someone, but asking them to remain available

An unusual offer: The company has decided to terminate your employment for economic reasons. However, we'd like to be able to continue to draw on your advice and expertise for the next six months. In addition to a generous severance package, which you'll find outlined in this memo, we're willing to provide you with continued use of your office and secretary for up to six months, and we will characterize your departure in any manner you'd like.

Angry: *Exactly why would I want to help out the company that has just fired me?*

Quid pro quo: Because the package we're offering you is far more generous than you'd otherwise receive. After all, the law doesn't require any severance at all.

Negotiates: *In addition to use of my office I'd like you to pick up the cost of my COBRA for those same six months. In addition, I'll be free to leave whenever I land another position.*

Agree: Agreed. If at the end of six months you're still available and we still require your help, we'll be willing to discuss continuing the arrangement. And if you land another position and we still need your help, we can talk about a part-time consulting fee.

Negotiate: We won't be able to pick up the cost of COBRA, but we can increase the severance payment by 20 percent. If at the end of six months you're still available, and we still require your help, we'll be willing to discuss continuing the arrangement And if you land another position and we still need your help, we can talk about a part-time consulting fee.

unemployed. No matter what the circumstances, someone will always ask, "If they're as good as they appear, why were they fired?" I suggest that if you're terminated but asked to remain available, you try to negotiate continued employment. In effect, ask them to defer your termination.

You're not looking to reverse the decision. You're simply asking for the company to keep you on the books as a full-time employee until an agreed-upon date when they will no longer need you to be available. As part of this discussion you can reach an agreement on your future severance package. While you're still employed you can actively look for another job and honestly say that you still have a job, making you a more attractive candidate.

If this effort doesn't work, your fallback position can be negotiating the best possible "consulting" arrangement. See Workscript 3.10.

Making an End Run

Going over your boss's head is the single most dangerous thing you can do as an employee. You are saying, both by your request and any subsequent actions, that you do not accept your manager's superiority over you. You are directly challenging his or her authority. Sure, you could maneuver your manager into saying he or she is okay with your talking to his or her boss, and questioning or appealing a decision. But saying it and meaning it are two completely different things. (The exception is when your manager is also a friend and actively encourages you to make the end run after reluctantly firing you.)

Whatever the outcome of this effort, you have forever damaged your working relationship with this person and perhaps the company. Your boss's boss will be no less a believer in the chain of command than your own manager. He or she doesn't want authority challenges, and will be loathe to countenance, let alone encourage them. But let's say you achieve the miraculous and win your appeal. You could come back after winning a reversal and be greeted by your boss with congratulations on both your initiative and the outcome. But you have now moved to the top of the hit list. You're a dead man or woman walking. This is the ultimate no-win workplace situation.

That's why the only time you should try an end run is when you have either actually or effectively been terminated. In that case, it's a no-lose situation. Whenever a manager pulls the trigger and terminates you, he or she has used the ultimate weapon in the workplace arsenal. What more can the company do to you? It can't give you a bad recommendation—out of fear of liability, companies don't say anything about former employees today, other than verifying employment. Having offered you an inadequate severance package in exchange for your signing a termination agreement, it can't take back that offer simply in response to your appealing it.

Even if you're unsuccessful in your appeal, you'll gain some psychic rewards. You'll be able to look back with no regrets. You'll have stood up for yourself and left no stone unturned in fighting back. If nothing else, you'll regain a feeling of empowerment you might otherwise have lost if you didn't fight back with everything you had.

The secret to making the end run is presenting it, not as a request, but as an announcement. You're not asking for permission, you're simply showing the courtesy of letting your ex-manager know what you're doing.

Then, if your boss's boss voices any objection to violating the chain of command, use all the guilt you can generate to force him or her to listen to your pitch. Once again, you've got nothing to lose and everything to gain. Having pushed this far, you need to keep pushing until every option is exhausted. Force this individual to hear you out before rejecting your appeal. See Workscript 3.11.

Workscript 3.10 Being terminated, but asked to remain available

An unusual offer: *The company has decided to terminate your employment for economic reasons. However, we'd like to be able to continue to draw on your advice and expertise for the next six months. In addition to a generous severance package, which you'll find outlined in this memo, we're willing to provide you with continued use of your office and secretary for up to six months, and will characterize your departure in any manner you'd like.*

Defer terminaton: *That's a very interesting suggestion. However, why don't we simply defer my termination for six months. We can agree on a termination agreement and a severance package now which won't take effect until a date in the future. Meanwhile, I'll be completely available for you.*

Can't do it: *I'm afraid we can't do that. The best we can do is create a kind of consulting package for you.*

Negotiates: In that case, in addition to use of my office I'd like you to pick up the cost of my COBRA for those same six months. In addition, I'll be free to leave whenever I land another position.

Don't have power: *I don't have the power to make that kind of decision. I'd have to speak to Mr. Big about it.*

If you don't receive an acceptable response, turn to Workscript 3.11 on page 66.

Workscript 3.11 Making an end run around your boss

Announce end run: I understand what you're saying. However, I think there are extenuating circumstances in my case. I couldn't live with myself without speaking to Ms. Big directly. This has nothing to do with you and me, it's just something I felt compelled to do.

Later that day, meeting with your boss's boss

An overt approach: It's important to me that you know my supervisor knows of my coming here to speak with you. I believe my situation is unique, and addressing it in a fair and equitable manner requires the involvement of someone at a higher level, such as yourself.

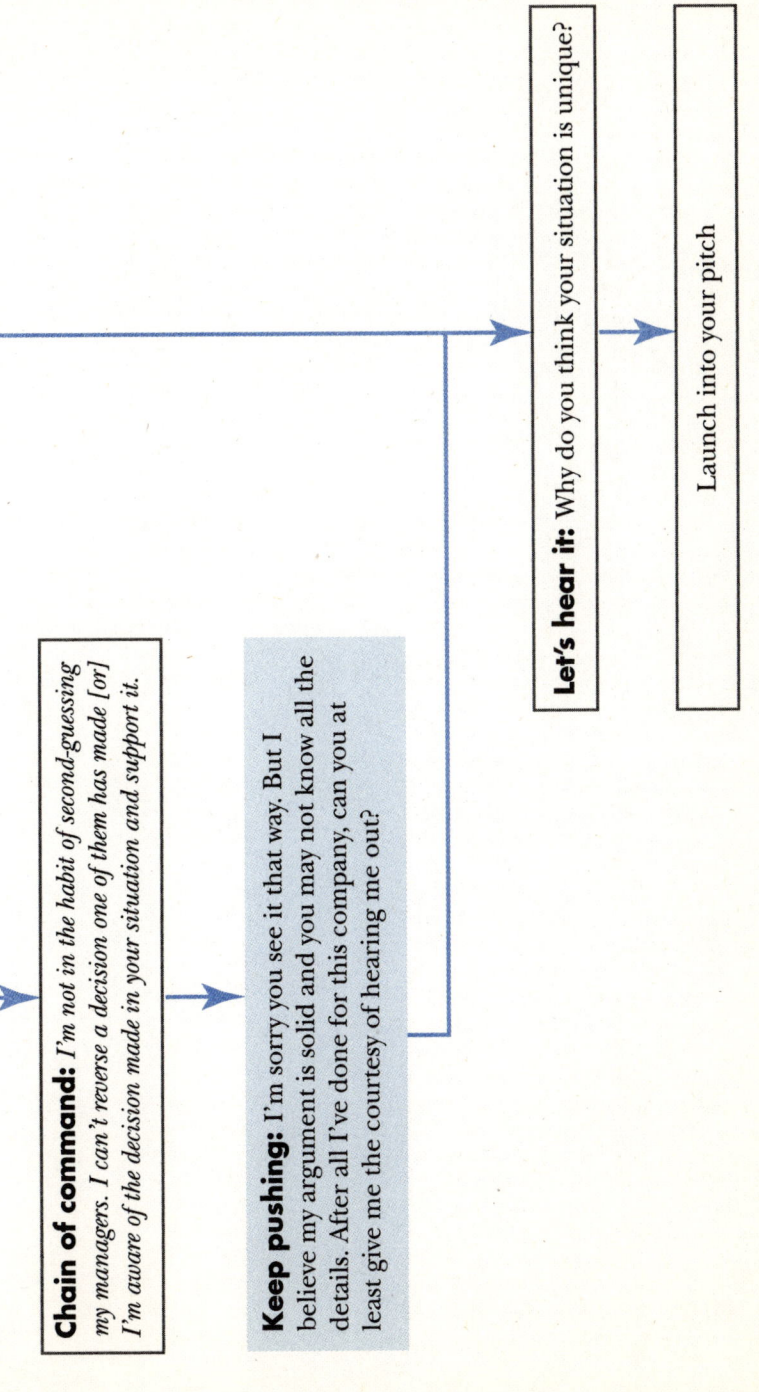

Chapter 4

EMPLOYER COST-CUTTING

Asking employees to make sacrifices is not as difficult as it used to be. In years past you might need to appeal to abstract notions such as company loyalty and career development to mitigate the anger and minimize the resistance with which such initiatives would be met. Today, these dialogues need not be cloaked as appeals and there's less necessity of placating feelings.

In a difficult job market these discussions become presentations of fact; less dialogue and more declaration. Though it's an uncomfortable metaphor, these discussions today take on all the trappings of extortion. Employees are made offers they cannot refuse without losing their job. Still, employers shouldn't offer a hint of apology or make a request for assent. You don't have to hide the fact that you're informing, not requesting. Employee sacrifices and cut-backs are today's efforts at maintaining company health and individual employment. It's unnecessary to even hint at what should be obvious:

for the employee the alternative to accepting this change is unemployment.

Any employee who today responds to these changes, however draconian, with an instant resignation, is someone who already has a foot out the door anyway, and is just looking for an excuse to leave. That isn't to say you won't lose people in the long term. Recognize that by changing the terms of employment you are really forcing people to launch job searches. Those who can find a position with conditions better than those you've just imposed will leave. That's the risk when an employer is resorting to extortion.

These efforts will be less shocking today than they would have been in years past, since employees now have little or no trust in employers. Asking for sacrifices will be seen as merely one more example of the increased uncertainty of work. Because short-term results are now all that matter, employee arguments about past practices and prior performance carry less weight. The answer, bluntly, is "That was then and this is now."

The degree to which employees understand that jobs and careers now have expiration dates could make them more accepting of whatever change you must make to the nature of their job. A veteran employee who realizes that his or her job is near extinction will be less resistant to change. And since it's these very veterans who are most often the targets of cutbacks, it's possible you could avoid long-term morale problems.

In the short term, the rarity of face-to-face communication today can also help lessen the impact of the blow. The moment you ask someone to come in to speak with you, they will assume the worst. Presenting them with almost any scenario that's short of immediate termination could actually be received with relief.

Taking advantage of this "relief effect" is one reason to hold all these discussions as one-on-one dialogues. Another reason is that such meetings allow for details to be discussed privately. That could give prideful employees a chance to save face. Finally, by avoiding group discussions of employee sacrifices, you minimize the chances of dissension spreading. In a group setting, all it takes is one person voicing complaints for others to feel more comfortable airing their gripes, as well.

Since these sacrifices can have profound, perhaps immediate personal impact, but not necessarily instant workplace impact, the best day to announce them is Friday. This provides employees with a weekend in which to talk to family members. Have the discussions after lunch to minimize the amount of work time lost to commiserating and gossip.

Furloughs without Pay

Any company that is facing a temporary downturn in revenues, or a short-term cash flow crisis, can potentially weather the storm by furloughing employees without pay. As a rule, furloughs should be no shorter than one week and no longer than a month: shorter than one week, and the potential savings aren't worth the effort; longer than a month is blatantly unfair. Businesses cannot expect employees furloughed for more than a month to ever return. In that situation you might as well fire the employee and then look to rehire when the company can afford to re-staff.

You must have a fixed return date established before you break the news. Without a set return, it's a termination, not a furlough. Unless the furlough is the result of a sudden emergency, you should provide some advance warning. If the leave is going to be of one or two weeks duration, you should provide a minimum of one week's notice to allow for him or her to make whatever financial arrangements they can. If the leave is going to be of more than two weeks, do your best to provide a month's notice, since the arrangements will be more problematic. Make the announcement on a Friday to provide an added two days of time to make arrangements and eliminate as much on-the-job unhappiness as possible.

It's vital that you provide as honest an assessment about the extent and composition of the furlough as you can. You have to assume that news about who is being furloughed and who isn't will spread throughout the company, whether it's supposed to be closely held information or not. To maintain what little credibility you have as an employer in today's environment, it's important you don't make false or misleading statements.

Explain that the furlough is an effort to keep the company from getting into trouble, rather than a way of getting out of already-existing trouble. The alternative isn't the status quo, it's termination.

Point out that, while a burden, the furlough isn't unfair. Unfair would be asking people to work for no pay. In that spirit, you can't agree to any exceptions, even in special circumstances. See Workscript 4.1.

If you're called in and told you're being furloughed without pay, you need to focus on minimizing the potential harm to your personal finances. You can assume that rather than being singled out, you're just the first in a cycle of furloughs, since the company can't furlough everyone at once and stay in business. After all, if you were a singular target you'd have been fired, not furloughed.

One alternative you can propose is that, rather than taking two weeks off without pay, you could work half-time at half-pay for four weeks. While the total economic impact is identical, spreading a smaller cut over a longer period of time can be easier to absorb personally. Another option to consider is to offer to give up your two weeks of paid vacation. The long-term effect will be the same for your employer. Not interrupting your cash flow may be more important than two weeks of relaxation.

Decide which of these two options you'd prefer, and propose that first. If you're turned down, propose the other option. If that too is rejected, give up the effort. Making an end run to a higher authority could put your long-term employment in jeopardy. See Workscript 4.2.

Full-Time Jobs Becoming Part-Time Jobs

Jobs don't become extinct overnight. Many businesses act that way, however, waiting until a position makes zero economic sense, and then firing the individual who held the job. A more sensible, and perhaps more humane response, is to act more quickly but less drastically. The moment it becomes clear that a position is becoming less necessary, it can be reclassified as a part-time rather than full-time job.

It's important to realize that doing this to an employee, while less painful than immediate termination, represents a traumatic shift in the terms of employment. Very few employees will be able to function on such a dramatic cut in their earned income. A handful who are devoted to their job, for one reason or another, will look to supplement this now part-time job with another part-time stream of income. Most will simply start looking for another full-time job, using the free time they now have to do their job hunting. Some may actually request termination instead in order to search for a new job full time. In that case you should provide them with the same severance package they'd receive if you were terminating them.

Even though odds are high that you'll eventually lose your current employee, it's worth making the effort to keep him or her in place for as long as possible, rather than just firing and then rehiring a new part-timer. You have someone who knows the job and, presumably, is good at it. Hiring someone new involves a cost and a risk you may as well defer for as long as possible.

Workscript 4.1 Furloughing someone without pay

Time off without pay: The company is furloughing you without pay for two weeks. The furlough will start one week from this coming Monday. This is based entirely on economic factors and is no reflection on how we feel about you or your performance.

Fear: *How am I supposed to get by without a paycheck? [or] I've got my kid's tuition bill coming due this month.*

Trouble: *Does this mean the company is in trouble?*

Unfair: *This really is unfair of the company.*

Up to you: We've given you advance warning so you can explore all your options for dealing with this furlough. This is a short-term measure to insure our jobs are safe in the long term.

Avoid trouble: Actually it's some of our customers who are in trouble. We're taking this step in the short term to keep our company healthy and our jobs safe in the long term.

Not unfair: It would be unfair if we were asking you to work without pay. The alternative to this is permanent job loss for some of us. This is a short-term measure to keep our jobs safe in the long term.

Just me: *Is everyone in the company being furloughed, or is it just me?* → **Selective:** We're staggering the furloughs over the next two months so the company can continue to operate. This is a short-term measure to ensure our jobs are safe in the long term.

Accusatory: *Are you being furloughed, too?* → **Don't engage:** No. Not on this round. This is a short-term measure to keep all our jobs safe in the long term.

Workscript 4.2 Being furloughed without pay

Time off without pay: *The company is furloughing you without pay for two weeks. The furlough will start one week from this coming Monday. This is based entirely on economic factors and is no reflection on how we feel about you or your performance.*

Give up vacation: Two weeks without pay will be very painful for me and my family. I understand the economic necessity, but what if rather than furloughing me, I give up my vacation and work for those two weeks. That will provide the company with an equal savings without hurting our productivity in any way.

Spread out the pain: Two weeks without any pay will be very painful for me and my family. I understand the economic necessity, but what if I work half time, at half pay for four weeks instead. That will provide the company with an equal savings with less of an impact on productivity and less of a shock to my family's finances.

Try to give at least one month's notice before the change takes place. That gives the employee a chance to make whatever personal arrangements they can to compensate for the cut in income. It is likely they'll also use this time to look for another job. That's only fair.

Hold this conversation after lunch on a Monday, giving the employee a chance to start working on their financial options right away. See Workscript 4.3.

There's no way around it: if your full-time job is suddenly turned into a part-time job you are, for all intents and purposes, being fired. No employer can realistically expect someone who relied on a full-time income to suddenly be able to cope with a part-time income. And no employer can assume a suddenly part-time employee will be able to find a second part-time job that fits his or her now altered schedule. The employer is trying to have it's cake and eat it, too: eliminate a full-time position, but keep the person who has been doing the job well for as long as possible.

There's no point in trying to argue them out of their decision. If they desperately wanted to keep you, they would have fired someone else and moved you into their place. And if there were some way to expand your job's responsibilities in order to keep it full-time, they would have just added to your workload. They've reached a decision they're not going to change.

Rather than debating, I suggest you respond in a similar manner, in terms of wanting to have the best of both worlds. Explain that this is, in effect, a termination, so ask for a severance package. Then, add that you would be happy to fill in as a part-timer for as long as they need you up until you land a new full-time position elsewhere. Your part-time pay, however long it lasts, will be a good supplement to your severance. Since they knew you'd only probably remain with them long enough to find a new job, your being a temporary part-timer won't be a surprise. And they had to be prepared for a severance request from the moment they conceived the plan. You're just suggesting they do both. See Workscript 4.4.

Workscript 4.3 Turning a full-time employee into a part-timer

Position, not you: I'm afraid the company has decided your position will be part time, starting one month from today. The economy [or] market simply doesn't justify your job being full time anymore. I want to stress this has nothing to do with you. We're happy with your performance and want to keep you. This is about your position, not you.

Can't get by: *I'm not going to be able to get by on a part-time income.*

Actually a termination: *In effect, you're firing me. Can I just get a severance package?*

Implores: *I can't believe this. I've always gotten great reviews. No one has ever said there was anything wrong with my work.*

Benefits: *How will this effect my benefits package? I can't afford to lose my insurance as well.*

78

→ **Your problem:** We understood that was a possibility. If you can't get by, you'll have to do your best to find some way to subsidize your stream of income. We'd understand if you got a second part-time job.

→ **Okay:** I understand your feelings. While we'd like to keep you, if you want to leave immediately we can give you a severance package consisting of . . . .

→ **Not you:** Your work has been excellent. That's why we want to keep you. This has nothing to do with you. It's your position that's the problem. We simply can't justify it as a full-time job any longer.

→ **No change:** We've decided you will be able to keep your current benefits package for as long as you work here. It wouldn't be right to scale back your benefits as well.

Workscript 4.4 Being asked to become a part-time employee

Position, not you: *I'm afraid the company has decided your position will be part time, starting one month from today. The economy [or] market simply doesn't justify your job being full time anymore. I want to stress this has nothing to do with you. We're happy with your performance and want to keep you. This is about your position, not you.*

This is a termination: *Obviously I'm terribly disappointed. This amounts to a termination since there's no way I can support my family on a part-time income, and it's highly unlikely I'd be able to find a second part-time job that fits with this job's schedule. Therefore I'd like you to provide me the kind of severance package you would have made available if you were simply terminating me without cause. However, I am sympathetic to your need for continuity, so I'd be willing to fill the part-time position at the reduced salary for either as long as you need me or until I find another position. I think that could answer both our needs.*

Pay Cuts

Cutting pay can be an effective way to trim expenses without incurring the traumatic impact terminations have on morale. While it will never be a popular step, if salary cuts are framed as an attempt to preserve jobs, they'll be accepted by most.

Ironically, it's easier to cut pay across an entire department or company than it is to cut a single person's pay. That's because spreading the pain makes it clear this is an economic measure. No matter how fervent your denials, a person singled out for a pay cut will see it as an attack on their personal value.

Your goal in a department-wide cut is to mitigate damage to morale and get the team to focus on the job-saving nature of the cuts. Your goal in an individual cut is to convince the employee that this isn't personal, it's about the position that he or she holds, and to keep him or her on board. After all, if the employee wasn't effective, you'd be discussing termination, not a pay cut.

Department or company-wide reductions should be presented in a group meeting. Bringing in an entire department and announcing a comprehensive cut can have the ironic effect of increasing team togetherness: they are all sacrificing for each other. It also prevents the backstabbing that could result from a series of one-on-one meetings in which employees might offer up one of their coworkers as a sacrificial lamb. Cuts should be announced as soon as possible after the decision has been reached, so the news doesn't leak. Schedule the meeting for a Friday afternoon to avoid a week's worth of sulking. Cuts should take effect immediately to signal the urgency of the effort and to make it clear there's no flexibility. Explain that the situation will be reviewed in six months to see if the cuts can be restored. See Workscript 4.5.

Workscript 4.5 Cutting an entire staff's pay

Emergency job protection: For the health of the company and in order to protect everyone's jobs, the company has decided to institute an across-the-board 10 percent pay cut for the department. This is being done as an alternative to terminating someone. It will take effect with your next paycheck. We will reexamine the situation in six months to see if the cuts can be restored.

Every department? *Is every department being cut?*

In trouble? *Does this mean the company is in trouble? Should we start looking for new jobs?*

Last time? *Is this going to be the final cut or should we anticipate there will be more in the future?*

Other ways? *Couldn't the company find some other places to cut costs instead of cutting our pay?*

My review? *I was scheduled for my annual review in two months. Will that still take place?*

82

▶ **Truth:** Yes, it's across the entire company. [or] No, the cuts are limited to those departments whose revenues have shrunk dramatically.

▶ **Not now:** We're taking this step to keep the company out of trouble and protect all your jobs.

▶ **No more . . . for now:** We don't anticipate having to make any additional cuts down the road. However, no one knows what the future holds, so I can't make any promises.

▶ **None left:** The company believes it has exhausted every other cost-cutting opportunity, so the only thing left we could trim were either jobs or salaries. We've chosen to cut pay rather than fire individuals.

▶ **Reviews cancelled:** Performance reviews will continue but salary reviews are all cancelled until further notice.

Be completely truthful about the extent of the cuts, since the news will leak out eventually. If cuts are company-wide, say so. If they are limited to specific departments, explain why.

Individual pay cuts should be done in private. Most times the individuals targeted for pay cuts are the highest-paid, longest-serving employees. As a result, their self-identification with their jobs will be strong. That means their reactions may run from one extreme to another. Be prepared for some pushback and denial, but also grief and shame. Absorb anger to the extent possible and offer to do what you can to help them save face.

When cutting an individual's pay, it's wiser to have the dialogue early in the week and day to give them a chance to "get back on the horse" immediately, rather than stew at home over the evening or weekend. See Workscript 4.6.

Having your pay cut is painful and problematic, but . . . it's not as bad as being fired. That's what you need to keep in mind when you're told your salary is being trimmed. Rather than being antagonistic, self-pitying, or obsequious, try to use whatever guilt exists as leverage to mitigate the harm to your stream of income.

One possibility is to ask for the pay cut to be phased in gradually, rather than take effect all at once. That will give you a better chance to adjust your personal finances. Another option is to use this as a rationale for a flex-time arrangement. Offer to work the same amount of time, but to do it in four days rather than five. Suggest that the now free fifth day gives you an opportunity to make up for the cut in your income.

Choose whichever of these options makes the most sense for you. If you're turned down, don't make an end-run appeal. Your higher-than-typical salary put a target on your back and resulted in this pay cut. Now that your salary is in line with the pack, that target has been removed. Go over your boss's head and the target reappears, even larger than before. By all means, try to mitigate the damage of this cut, but if you fail, accept it and surreptitiously start looking for a new job. See Workscript 4.7.

Increasing Hours but Not Pay

Businesses in which increased hours on the job will result in increased revenue—such as a retailer—always have the option of asking employees to work increased hours without additional pay, in order to boost their bottom lines.

While you can present this effort as an alternative to cutting pay or firing someone, employees are unlikely to be supportive of the effort. Despite its more dire impact, pay cuts and terminations are perceived by employees as emergency defensive measures, whereas extending working hours is perceived as a money grab by management. Regardless of how well it's explained, this effort will always generate resentment. The best you can hope for is to make the case and keep overt grumbling to a minimum.

This should be done in a group and at the end of the workweek. Try to give at least one or two weeks' notice to allow employees to make whatever arrangements are needed to deal with longer working hours. Be prepared to absorb the inevitable pushback and anger. If the situation allows for some flexibility in terms of when in the workweek the hours are added, do what you can to accommodate people. See Workscript 4.8.

Expanding Responsibility without Increasing Pay

One way to save money in trying economic times is to stop farming out work to vendors and bring the tasks in-house. By expanding the responsibilities of a current employee to

Workscript 4.6 Cutting an individual employee's pay

Salary doesn't work: The company has decided it needs to cut your salary. This has nothing to do with the quality of your work or how we feel about you as an employee. It's simply that the job you do for us is no longer worth what you're being paid. In this marketplace we believe your position should be paid 10 percent less than you're currently receiving. As a result, your salary will be reduced to that level effective with your next paycheck.

In trouble? *Does this mean my job is in trouble?*

Hasn't listened: *I don't understand. My reviews have been excellent for years.*

Just me? *Is anyone else having their pay cut.*

Angry: *Is this how the company rewards 20 years of loyalty and hard work?*

Embarrassed: *Will you be telling the rest of the staff about this?*

▶ **Not now:** Your job would be in trouble if we don't make this cut. We're doing this because we want to keep you.

▶ **Not about you:** This has nothing to do with you or your performance. It's about your position. It simply isn't worth what we're currently paying.

▶ **Just you:** Not in this department. You're the highest paid staffer and as a result, you're the only one whose salary now doesn't match the value of the job.

▶ **Not about loyalty:** This has nothing to do with loyalty. It's about the marketplace. We're doing this in order to keep you because of what a great employee you've been.

▶ **Private:** The only other people who know about this are senior management and the payroll department.

Workscript 4.7 Having your pay cut

Salary doesn't work: *The company has decided it needs to cut your salary. This has nothing to do with the quality of your work or how we feel about you as an employee. It's simply that the job you do for us is no longer worth what you're being paid. In this marketplace we believe your position should be paid 10 percent less than you're currently receiving. As a result, your salary will be reduced to that level effective with your next paycheck.*

Cut me gradually: Obviously I'm not happy with the decision but I'm glad this isn't based on me or my performance. Because this will have a dramatic impact on my personal finances, it would be helpful if you could make the transition a gradual process, say, cutting my salary 2 percent per month for the next 5 months. That will give me a better chance to make the personal adjustments necessary.

Flex-time option: Obviously I'm not happy with the decision but I'm glad this isn't based on me or my performance. Because this will have a dramatic impact on my personal finances, I'd like the chance to make up what you're taking from me. I'd like to do the same job I'm doing now, working the same number of hours, but in four days rather than five. This will give me a chance to make up for the pay cut. If after a trial period you don't feel the arrangement is working, we can return to a five-day schedule, but I think it only fair to give the flex-time option a try.

include work previously done by an outsider, without increasing his or her pay, a business can cut expenses without cutting salaries, while offering a growth opportunity to a promising individual.

This shift must be presented, not as a matter for debate, but as a certain step. The added burden should be framed as both a means of keeping the employee's salary at its current level, and an opportunity for him or her to grow professionally.

Obviously, this conversation should be held one on one with the person whose portfolio is being expanded. The specific timing of the conversation is less important than that it is held far enough in advance, allowing the individual to tidy up their current schedule, but near enough the change for it to clearly appear inevitable. While every situation has its own unique circumstances, one week's warning would be a good general rule.

Having been called into your office for a private meeting, the employee will be fearing termination. When they find out they're being given more work, not being fired, it will come as a relief. It's unlikely you'll get direct pushback since you are, presumably, dealing with one of your top performers who is apt to be more savvy than confrontational. Instead, you'll probably hear about scheduling problems. In addition, you're apt to field questions intended to either plant the seed for future pay increases or minimize expectations. See Workscript 4.9.

If your workload or responsibilities are increased without a corresponding increase in pay, there's really nothing you can do to either fight it or seek redress without weakening your hold on the job. You can perhaps reduce expectations, and maybe plant the seeds for future opportunities, but otherwise all you can do is smile, say thank you, and accept that you're now probably going to have to work harder for longer hours. See Workscript 4.10.

Workscript 4.8 Increasing employee's hours but not pay

Working hours expanded: The company has decided to extend our business hours. In two weeks' time we will start staying open 40 rather than 35 hours a week. The reason for the extended hours is to generate sufficient additional revenue so that we can maintain our current salary and staffing levels. The company has chosen to do this instead of cutting pay or firing someone.

Angry: *Do we have any choice about this?*

Schedule problem: *But I need to pick up my daughter from day care.*

Flexibility? *Can we add the five hours to our schedule any way we'd like?*

Do this already: *I don't look at the clock. I'm already putting in extra time.*

→ **No:** Not if you want to maintain your position. The alternative isn't the status quo; it's pay cuts or terminations.

→ **Your problem:** We know this may force some of you to make changes in your personal schedules. That's why we're giving you some advance notice. This is something you'll have to work out on your own.

→ **Case by case:** We're not opposed to working out case-by-case arrangements for how you add the extra five hours. If your idea works for the company, we'll be open to it.

→ **Now not optional:** We realize many of you put in extra hours voluntarily, and we appreciate it. We're not making it mandatory for everyone.

Workscript 4.9 Extending responsibilities without increasing pay

Making your job bigger: The company has decided to make your job bigger. In order for us to keep paying your current salary, we need you to take on additional responsibilities. Starting one week from today we'll no longer be using the bookkeeping service and instead, you'll be taking charge of that role in addition to your current responsibilities.

No time: *I already put in an enormous number of hours. I don't know how I'm going to fit this in as well.*

Future raise? *Will I be eligible for an increase in the future because of this?*

Just me? *Is anyone else taking on additional responsibilities?*

Permanent? *Is this a permanent expansion of my responsibilities or just a temporary economic measure?*

Downplay expectations: *I appreciate the vote of confidence but I'm not sure how quickly I can pick this up.*

We know: We know how hard, and well you work. That's why we want to keep you, and keep paying you your current salary. We have confidence you'll be able to handle this as well.

No promises: We can't promise you anything about increases, but taking on added responsibility certainly increases your value to the company. The more valued someone is, the more secure their position and, potentially, the greater their reward.

Just the top people: We're asking this of only our top people, those we think capable of doing more in the short and long term.

Don't know: We can't make a judgment on the long term, but I can tell you that this change is for the foreseeable future.

We're confident: We considered this carefully and we have the utmost confidence in your ability to do the job. We know there will be a learning curve and we're comfortable with that.

Workscript 4.10 Having your responsibilities increased but not your pay

Making your job bigger: *The company has decided to make your job bigger. In order for us to keep paying your current salary, we need you to take on additional responsibilities. Starting one week from today, we'll no longer be using the bookkeeping service and instead, you'll be taking charge of that role in addition to your current responsibilities.*

Thanks for the vote of confidence: Thank you for this vote of confidence. While I've never actually been in charge of the bookkeeping process before, I promise you I'll do my very best to do as good a job with that as I do with the rest of my work. I'm willing to take on whatever the company needs, today and in the future.

Staff Reductions

It is usually best to have the individual who directly leads a work team be the one to choose whom to fire, and then do the actual termination. The man or woman on the spot is apt to have the best understanding of which employee is either at the bottom of the performance range or whose absence will have the least negative impact on the team. In addition, their personal relationship with the employee being let go could provide a modicum of human warmth to an awkward and painful situation.

The exceptions to this rule are when you fear that nepotism or favoritism may play a role in the selection of who to let go, or when the team leader voices extreme trepidation about pulling the trigger.

Having been called into your office, the team leader will have a moment of relief that it's not him or her being let go, but that will quickly be replaced by apprehension. No one wants to fire somebody. Everyone dreads the act, even if they've been forced to do it dozens of times in a long management career. So dismay is to be expected and usually worked through. However, you as the higher-level manager are ultimately responsible for the process. If the team leader is so shaken you fear he or she will not be able to do the job professionally, then it's in your and the to-be-terminated employee's best interests that you do it yourself.

Be prepared to give some broad guidelines for both the selection and the actual act of termination. It's a given that losing a staff person will have some negative impact on productivity and morale. The idea is for the team leader to select the individual whose loss will have the least and briefest impact. Give them sufficient time to make a reasoned choice—at least a week—but caution them that any leak could be disastrous to the entire team's morale.

Most human resources departments have instructional materials on how to conduct a termination. But if such

Workscript 4.11 Reducing an employee's staff

You have to let someone go: Management has determined we need to cut back. We've explored all the options and have decided you have to cut your staff down by one person. I need you to think about who you'll be letting go, come back to me with your decision, and then let them know. The company will give you the discretion to provide anywhere from one to three week's severance, but please be prudent with those funds.

Incapable: *Oh my God! I don't think I can do this. I'v never fired anyone. These are all my friends. I just can't do it.*

Immature: *I don't know how we're going to manage with one less person. We're already stretched thin and now it will become impossible.*

Alternative? *Isn't there some other way we could cut back? Is there any way we could delay this?*

Suggestion: *I realize we need to cut back. What if instead of farming out the publicity work, we take that in-house? The money we save would be about the same as the salary of one of my people.*

If you can't: I think it would be more humane if you did it, but if you really aren't capable of this I will do it. Get back to me with your thoughts about who should be cut.

Deal with it: You will deal with it the way everyone else in the company is dealing with it: by working harder. That's the price we all are paying to keep the company healthy and our own jobs secure.

No: There's no other way that we've found. The decision has been made and it's up to you to carry it out without delay.

Good idea: That's a very interesting suggestion. Take some time this afternoon to prepare a memo on the idea and I'll bring it upstairs and see if it's an acceptable alternative.

Instructions: Here's a memo that has been prepared by human resources offering guidance on the best way to conduct a termination. The points I think are most important are that you make it clear the decision is irrevocable, that there's no appeal, and that it's been made solely for economic reasons. If you need any advice on this, feel free to ask.

material isn't available, offer some tips. Explain that it's vital the decision be presented as being absolutely irrevocable; there is no appeal or delay available. Note that the only reason for termination that isn't open to debate is economic necessity. Point out that it's usually best to fire someone on a Monday because he or she can then file for unemployment benefits and launch their job search right away. Give them instructions on the severance range available and ask them to be prudent.

Expect some pushback on the need for cutting staff. Besides the personal fear of the process and the potential impact on overall team performance, it's natural for the team leader to see a staff cut as a diminution of his or her own power and status, and to fight against it.

Even though they're expected, perhaps even reflexive, don't automatically dismiss the arguments that the team leader may raise against the firing, especially if they are issues you haven't previously considered. One reason you're turning to this team leader to select and execute the staff cut is because he or she has superior knowledge of the personnel and issues. This same superior knowledge could offer an informed alternative that you and other higher-level managers could not foresee.

Your goal is to prepare this individual to make a sound decision and conduct the termination in a humane and professional manner. See Workscript 4.11.

Whenever you're asked to cut your staff, you owe it to your employees and yourself to make the best argument you can to preserve the position. Just be sure your case is based on practical business reasons rather than on emotions. But if you can't change your own boss's mind about the advisability of cutting your staff, don't prolong the fight. Instead, accept it, but ask that in recognition of the added responsibilities and burden that will result, you receive an improved title. A title costs your employer nothing, but can be valuable to you when you ask for an increase or look for another job. See Workscript 4.12.

Workscript 4.12 Having your staff cut

You have to let someone go: *Management has determined we need to cut back. We've explored all the options and have decided you have to cut your staff by one person. We've explored all the options and your decision, and then let them know. The company will give you the discretion to provide anywhere from one to three week's severance, but please be prudent with those funds.*

→

Make your best practical business argument against a staff cut.

→

I can do it: *I understand and respect your decision. I can do this without it impacting quality, but it will require my being much more hands-on as well as providing an even greater degree of supervision. In recognition of this, I think it would be fair if I received a better title that more accurately reflects my expanded role.*

99

Workscript 4.13 Reducing an employee's budget

You have to find some cuts: Upper management has decided that due to the economic conditons we all have to cut back. I need you to cut your budget by ten percent [or] by $10,000. You're the expert on your team so I'm looking to you to come up with the savings. Quality and productivity cannot be impacted by these cuts since we need to at least maintain, if not increase, sales levels. Come back to me in a week with a new proposed budget.

There's no fat: *I just don't see how I can come up with that level of savings. We've already cut all the fat.*

I think quality will suffer: *Our vendors are already griping to me about their not making any money, and if I push the staff further, morale could really suffer. I don't know that we can cut back without it hurting our product.*

I know quality will suffer: *I'm always looking for places we can save and have implemented lots of internal measures. The only option we'd have in house would be to cut one position, and that would automatically cut our output by ten percent. Externally we could buy less expensive raw materials, but the difference in quality is pronounced, and I think our customers would be disappointed and look elsewhere.*

Find some: I know this won't be easy, but it's part of your job. If there truly isn't any place to make cuts in the budget, we'll be forced to look at either staff or salary cuts. And none of us want to go there until we've exhausted every other possibility.

Explain reality: No one wants to cut back or work longer hours. We know that. But the alternative isn't the status quo, it's finding another vendor or cutting staff or salary. Cuts have to be made one way or another.

Get me some evidence: I understand your points. Draft a memo for me, outlining what you've told me, and get me a sample of the cheaper material. I'll take them both upstairs and see if I can convince them we have to look elsewhere for savings.

Budget Reductions

Perhaps the simplest and most effective way for a business to cut back in lean times is to mandate budget cuts from its departments and teams. While problematic, it's certainly nowhere near as traumatic as cutting staff or salaries. And while it's sure to earn some pushback, the reaction of those who are charged with cutting back and the impact on the morale of the rank and file won't be as dramatic.

Rather that insisting on specific cuts, it makes more sense to provide general guidelines and ask the manager or team leader to come up with the specifics. He or she is the expert on his bailiwick. Besides, handing over the selection of cuts reinforces the individual's perceived power and authority, which will probably take a hit from any budget cut.

Provide an amount or percentage goal, insist that neither quality nor productivity decline, and set a deadline for submission of the new budget. You want to look at the proposed cuts yourself before they're enacted to make sure they won't have a negative impact. If they can convince you that any budget cut will necessarily result in a loss of sales, you'll need to rethink the idea. Otherwise, objections and protestations should be brushed aside with an insistence that finding nonhurtful savings is part of their job. See Workscript 4.13.

In trying economic times, you have to expect that you'll be asked to trim spending. It's a given that you'll need to come up with savings that don't hurt quality, even if it requires you and your team working harder and for longer hours. Rather than pushing back, embrace the responsibility and stress your willingness to do whatever it takes to help the company. See Workscript 4.14.

Workscript 4.14 Having your budget reduced

You have to find some cuts: *Upper management has decided that due to the economic conditions we all have to cut back. I need you to cut your budget by 10 percent [or] by $10,000. You're the expert on your team, so I'm looking to you to come up with the savings. Quality and productivity cannot be impacted by these cuts since we need to at least maintain, if not increase, sales levels. Come back to me in a week with a new proposed budget.*

Thanks for the vote of confidence: I appreciate the confidence you have in my knowledge of our operations. Your request is something I've been anticipating and I have been thinking about some areas where we could potentially cut back. Rest assured we'll do everything we can to ensure that quality isn't impacted. I'll be back to you in a week with my ideas. Thanks again for the expression of confidence.

Chapter 5

ON BENDED KNEE

Ironically, the more difficult the economic environment, the more seriously you need to take employee requests. While you may have a ready reason to say *no* any time an employee comes to you on bended knee, that could cost the company more in the long run. That's because these requests carry more than the usual import for the employee.

It's safe to assume that the people working for you aren't stupid. They know what the job market is like and what the economic conditions are in your industry and organization. They know that asking for something at a time when business is down and when jobs are tough to find isn't just an uphill struggle, it's potentially dangerous. The natural and common reaction would be to not shake the boat, to refrain from making any request until conditions improve.

Yet, despite all that, here they are, asking you for something. That means this request is extraordinarily important to them. This isn't a reflexive action. They're not indulging a whim. They are coming to you, putting themselves in danger, and asking you to do something that flies in the face of conventional wisdom. They have thought about this long and hard and have determined it is so important that it's worth the risk. If you respond flippantly or automatically to this kind of courageous effort, you're likely to alienate just the kind of employee you want to keep. Remember, even in times when the job market is flooded with unemployed workers it still costs a substantial sum to replace someone. And there is no guarantee that a new hire will be as good at the job as an existing employee. In fact, it's almost certain there will be at least some drop-off for however long it takes a new hire to adjust to a new environment.

Of course, when money is tight, you need to freeze, perhaps even cut costs. You don't want to do anything that will cost you or the company more money. Your goal, therefore, is to keep the company's expenses low by turning down costly requests, while at the same time placating the employee for whom the request is very important, so he or she neither leaves nor decreases work effort. One note of caution: While you have to lean toward not spending any more money, try to keep a mind that's at least ajar, if not open, to ideas. Good ideas may make sense in even the toughest economic times. In situations when a request is based on personal needs, you also want to keep any concessions on your part from turning into company-wide precedents.

In general, there are a number of strategies you can use to try to accomplish these goals. First, you can look for something without financial cost that you can offer as a replacement for whatever it was that the employee requested. For example, if an employee asks you for a raise, you could offer an improved title instead. Second, you can acknowledge the validity of the request but explain that the timing is problematic and offer to consider the request again in the future. Acknowledging that the employee is deserving, in profuse terms, could soften the blow, particularly when attached to a promise to review the matter again. A third, possibly fall-back, strategy is to offer to make a one-time bonus payment to the employee. It's surprising how small an amount may be sufficient to make an employee feel appreciated, particularly at a time when he or she knows money is tight. This one-time payment will be far less costly than any ongoing reward, and will probably be less than it would cost you to run a help-wanted ad. There are also specific tactics that you can employ in response to particular requests.

Employee requests sometimes take the form of extortion. The most common example of employee extortion is when the employee receives a job offer and uses it as leverage to get a raise or promotion. In the short term, extortion shouldn't impact your response. Do what you can, within budgetary and organizational restraints, to keep a valued employee in place, whether he or she has another offer or not. The cost and risk of replacing a good employee often outweighs the cost of keeping them, particularly if you can offer noncash rewards. In the long term, however, extortion should lead you to take a fresh look at this employee. Whether the other job offer came unsolicited or after a job search, this employee now has to be considered a permanent flight risk. You have to be prepared from this point on for this employee to leave at any time. In principle, that's true for every employee who isn't under contract. But you now have evidence that this particular employee is ready and willing to bolt.

While neither the time nor place of this conversation is in your control, one thing you can do is indicate, through your manners and mannerisms, that you take the matter very seriously. Maintain eye contact as much as is appropriate. Lean forward when you're listening to the request. Nod your head as if in agreement. And express your sorrow at having to turn him or her down.

Raise Requests

If money isn't an issue, responding to a raise request is a simple negotiation in which the employee seeks to get a salary closer to the top of the market range for his or her position, and the employer seeks to offer a salary at the lower end of the range. Unfortunately, today money is not only an issue, it's often *the* issue impacting every business decision.

The way you respond to this request should be based on an analysis of both the individual employee and the dynamics of the team or department as a whole. This analysis will have to be done on the fly, since you'll have no control over the timing of this conversation. You can, of course, respond by asking for some time to think the matter over. However, that often results in lose-lose-lose results for the manager. By not acceding to the request at the time, you generate anger and disappointment. If you come back with a rejection, then that anger and disappointment will grow. If you come back with an effort at negotiation, it will be taken as a rejection that you're trying to soften, making your offers less attractive psychologically and emotionally. Even if you come back with an agreement, the response on some level will be "What took you so long?" It's usually better to make an on-the-spot analysis and render an immediate decision.

The argument the employee makes to justify an increase impacts how you respond.

If an employee suggests that he or she is due a raise simply because of their longevity, you can simply explain that such automatic raises are a thing of the past and just not part of today's workplace. You can soften the blow by suggesting that the employee could raise his or her value to the company by improved performance, which you're willing to evaluate at a date in the future, or by taking on additional responsibilities.

By taking over tasks which you are, for instance, farming out to a vendor, an employee can help him- or herself and the company at the same time.

If an employee argues that his or her salary doesn't reflect the market value for the role being performed, you need to be more solicitous. This is the classically correct argument for a raise. The implication is that the company would have to pay more to replace this employee, so in order to keep from having to pay the costs of a job search and a higher salary, as well as assuming the risk of an unproven employee, the company should simply bring the employee up to the level the market justifies. A sound argument to which the only real response is that the money simply isn't there right now. If you don't place a high value on this employee, as an alternative to money you can promise to review the matter in the future, or suggest taking on added responsibilities, as you would in response to a longevity argument. However, if you do value this individual, you should make more attractive counteroffers.

Begin by agreeing with the employee's assessment. Say they are valuable to the company and are worth every penny for which they're asking. But since the money isn't there right now, all you can do is offer them things other than a pay increase.

Time is often as valuable, if not more valuable, than money. That's particularly true for employees who have children or who may have an entrepreneurial streak. You can offer these employees flex-time or a telecommuting option as an alternative to a raise. Explain that if they believe they're able to get their work done in four days rather than five, you're willing to agree to a trial flex-time experiment. This would give the entrepreneurial employee a day to independently make the additional money they're seeking. Alternatively, explain that if they think they can get their work done at home one day a week, you're willing to give that a try.

For the employee with a long-term career vision, an improved title or position can be just as valuable as a raise. Not only will a better title or position set them up for a larger raise when money does become available, it will qualify them to look for higher-paying jobs out in the job market. The key here is not to create more problems than you solve by negatively impacting the dynamics of the department or group. You don't want to impact other employees negatively with this change . . . unless you're trying to send a message. If you're worried about how a promotion will impact the department, offer flex-time or telecommuting instead.

If offering time or an improved title isn't enough to satisfy a valued employee who isn't receiving market value, there's only one other sweetener you could offer: a cash bonus. A one-time payment, which has no impact on their ongoing salary, will cost far less than conducting a job search, and could be just the ego massage an employee needs. Insist on confidentiality, or else you'll find a line outside your door looking for similar bonuses.

The third and most troubling raise argument an employee can make is that he or she has received an offer from another potential employer. If you don't place a high value on this individual, wish them all the best and let them go. If you do value this employee and want to keep him or her on board, you need to make the same kind of counters you would to the employee who isn't getting market value: time or title, or, if that's not enough, a cash bonus. However, the moment this individual leaves your office you need to start making plans for his or her replacement, perhaps even drawing up lists of potential candidates. That's because his or her willingness to listen to another offer—solicited or unsolicited—and then tell you about it, shows beyond a doubt that he or she is prepared to leave at any moment. See Workscript 5.1.

The most effective way for you to get a raise, whatever the economic environment, is to get a new job. You are worth more to another company if, in addition to bringing with you your skills and abilities and contacts, you also are taking them away from a competitor. Even in the most dire economic times, most companies are happy to poach a rival's key people.

Many people use such an external offer as an opportunity to extort an equivalent increase from their existing employer. While this is almost always effective (after all, your employer sees your move to a competitor as a double loss in the same way the competitor sees your coming on board as a double win), it's a gambit that comes with a very large risk. Your employer, even while matching the outside offer, will almost certainly change his or her perception of you as an employee. Rightly or wrongly you will now be seen as being more of a flight risk than anyone else. As a result, you may find yourself number one on any future hit list.

In today's environment I believe you have two options. If the outside offer is sufficiently attractive, simply accept it and move on. If, however, there is some reason—perhaps location—why you'd prefer to stay with your current employer despite the increased risk that comes from successful extortion, you need to receive some kind of security guarantee.

However, to ask your current employer for not only a raise, but a contract or termination agreement, as well, is double extortion. Asking for the security assurance is apt to be perceived as a slap in the face. You're implying that you don't trust your employer not to retaliate. Truth is, you don't trust them, nor should you. But openly acknowledging the fact isn't going to go over well. The solution is to blame it all on the outside company. Say that their offer to you includes a termination agreement as well as a raise. There's no sense lying about this, since you really should insist on some kind of protection

Workscript 5.1 Responding to a raise request

Longevity: *You yourself have said I'm doing my job well. It has been 18 months since my last increase and I think I deserve a raise.*

Market value: *I've been doing some research and have found that the average salary in the industry for someone doing my job is 3 percent more than I'm currently earning. I believe my superior performance entitles me to an increase of at least that level.*

Extortion: *Acme, Inc., has offered me a position that pays more than I'm currently earning. All things being equal I'd like to stay here, but I have to consider my family's needs.*

Delay: Longevity isn't sufficient reason for a pay increase in today's economic environment. The best I can do for you is to promise to review your performance and pay in another six months. By then the financial situation may be different.

Do more: Longevity isn't sufficient reason for a pay increase in today's economic environment. If, on the other hand, you were willing to add the responsibility for bookkeeping to your current job description, an increase would be justified.

Time: You're a very valued employee and I'd like nothing more than to give you an increase. But the money simply isn't there right now. What if we were to agree to a flex-time [or] telecommuting arrangement instead?

Title: You're a very valued employee and I'd like nothing more to give you an increase. But the money simply isn't there right now. What if I was to name you assistant manager instead and promise to explore the pay issue again in another six months?

Insufficient: *I appreciate the offer but I really think I'm entitled to a higher salary [or] I really need you to at least match what Acme is offering me.*

Bonus too: We simply can't afford to increase your salary right now, but what if in addition to my previous suggestion we give you a one-time cash bonus of X?

when you're thinking of leaving a company you've been with for a long time in order to take a better job elsewhere.

If you're going to use an outside offer as leverage for a raise at your current job, the best time to have the discussion is early in the morning, before normal business hours. Don't schedule a specific appointment: that smacks of preplanning. Instead, show up at the manager's office unannounced, saying you have an important matter to discuss and asking for a few minutes. Rather than selecting a particular day of the week, have this conversation as soon after you receive the offer as possible. The more this appears to be a spontaneous event, the more likely your manager will believe it was unsolicited. See Workscript 5.2.

Promotion Requests

Most promotion requests today are based on past performance rather than future potential. Individuals who have survived a staff cut and have taken on additional responsibilities are coming to their managers some time later, and asking that they receive a new title or promotion that more accurately reflects what they're already doing. As a result, their argument is one of fairness, which, if true, is difficult to challenge.

In most cases, these requests don't center around a salary increase as well, since if that was their primary goal they'd be asking for a raise instead. That means the individual who asks for a raise is not only an acute observer of the economic environment, but is also someone who is thinking long term about their career, either at their current job or elsewhere. This can be an advantage, since it means they are likely to be open to other, perhaps less problematic, rewards that could help them to achieve the same goal.

The first step in responding is making an immediate judgment as to whether or not they have been doing a good enough job to merit such a promotion or title. If they haven't performed well, you can simply turn them down by providing a brief critique and offering to review them again, more formally, in six months' time.

If they are deserving of the title or promotion, you need to weigh the costs and benefits of acceding to their request. What will be the repercussions if you promote this person? How will others react?

If you don't believe there will be any real ramifications, then you can agree to the promotion while making it explicit that this does not automatically come with a pay increase.

If others might react poorly, you must ask yourself if it's worth more to keep this person happy and make others unhappy, or to make this person unhappy but keep others in the department happy. At times when the political costs might be too high to agree, you need to explain that the decision has nothing to do with them, but is instead based on external circumstances beyond their, and perhaps even your, control. In compensation, you can offer them an agreement to review the matter again soon and, if possible, offer a one-time cash bonus as a reward. See Workscript 5.3.

Today you can't ask for a promotion based on your excellent performance or your maturation. The only grounds that can't be denied in this environment is that your job profile has changed and that you have been doing well in carrying out your expanded responsibilities.

But even this unassailable argument can effectively be countered by explaining that promotions don't occur in a vacuum and that it's a decision based on outside factors which may be beyond the control of you and your manager. In that case, the best you can hope for is a promise of a future reconsideration and perhaps a bonus as a consolation prize.

Workscript 5.2 Requesting a raise

It's not my fault: Acme, Inc., has offered me a position which pays 10 percent more than I'm currently earning and includes a termination agreement giving me six months severance if I'm fired without cause. I haven't accepted it because I love it here and want to stay. But you know I have two kids preparing to go off to college. I need to put the needs of my family above my own wants. If you can match Acme's offer of an increase and six months guaranteed severance, I'll them them no and happily stay here.

Other than money: *You're a very valued employee and I'd like nothing more than to give you an increase. But the money simply isn't there right now. What if we were to agree to a flex time or telecommuting arrangement? [or] What if I were to name you assistant manager instead and promise to explore the pay issue again in another six months?*

Don't let the door hit you on the way out: *I wish you all the luck in the world over there. We simply can't give you a raise or a termination agreement.*

Raise yes, severance no: *Even though money is tight, I'm willing to meet thier salary offer to keep you on board. However, we have a company policy against giving employees contracts.*

Thanks, but no thanks: I appreciate your making an effort to keep me. But in today's environment there's no way I can pass up an opportunity to provide security for my family. I'm afraid that I can't turn down an offer that includes a termination agreement.

Workscript 5.3 Responding to a promotion request

I've earned it: *For the past eight months I've been doing the work that previously was done by the deputy manager. I think I've demonstrated that I'm more than capable and that I'm dedicated to the success of the company. I think it's only fair that, having proved myself, I be given the title of deputy manager.*

Not merited: The company is very grateful that you've taken on an expanded role and your efforts haven't gone unnoticed. However, we don't feel your current performance yet merits a formal promotion to the position. We believe you need to work further on your leadership and motivation of the rest of the staff. Let's review your performance again more formally six months from now and see how you've progressed.

No repercussions: You're absolutely right. You've done an excellent job and I should have come to you sooner about this. I'm only sorry that, along with your promotion to deputy manager I can't offer you a salary increase right now. However, that's something we can review again in the coming months. Congratulations.

Too many repercussions: You're absolutely right that you've proven you can do the job. You're doing very well. Unfortunately the timing simply isn't right for the company to make this move since it involves more than just you. What i can do is promise you to reexamine the issue in six months and to also provide you with a one-time cash bonus of $X as a thank you for all your excellent work.

Disappointed: *Thank you for the kind words, but I'm very disappointed. After all, I've done exactly what the company has asked and have excelled.*

When? *I understand what you're saying. Can you tell me when the timing will be right?*

Disappointed too: *I'm just as disappointed. I'd like nothing more than to give you the promotion, but the timing simply isn't right.*

No commitment: *You're asking me to make a prediction I can't make because it involves a company timetable. This decision isn't made in a vacuum. What I can do is promise to review the issue again in six months.*

Don't feel shy about asking for a bonus if it's not offered unprompted. This isn't in exchange for a future promotion, it's compensation for past efforts which otherwise will have gone unrewarded.

The best time to ask for a promotion is before normal business hours, when you 'will be most likely to get undivided attention. The earlier in the week you ask, the better, since fewer issues will have arisen to distract your manager. Make a specific appointment and bring along a memo that documents your presentation. Dress as you normally do. Don't shy away from direct eye contact, and try to project a sense of calm determination. Remember: Right is on your side. See Workscript 5.4.

Budget Increase Requests

It's the job of every manager, at every level of an organization, to look for opportunities to improve business and to watch for looming problems. Even in times of economic difficulty, your more astute employees could be coming to you with requests for budget increases, either to take advantage of something they've spotted or to avoid a problem they see on the horizon.

If you're approached with an idea to take advantage of an opportunity that requires additional budget allocations, you need to make a number of judgments. Is the idea a good one? Is sufficient money currently available? Does it make sense advocating to your own manager for additional funds? Even if the idea isn't something you think worth pursuing, you don't want to say that to your employee. It's important that you encourage this kind of initiative. Explain that the money simply isn't there right now, but praise their effort effusively. If the idea is a good one, but money isn't available, you should again praise the effort, but respond by sending

Workscript 5.4 Requesting a promotion

I've earned it: As you know, for the past eight months my job profile has expanded to include the responsibilities of deputy director. I believe I've demonstrated my ability to not only do the job, but do it well. Titles are important for my future career development, so I would like you to formally give me the title of deputy director.

Too many repercussions: *You're absolutely right that you've proven you can do the job. You're doing very well. Unfortunately the timing simply isn't right for the company to make this move, since it involves more than just you.*

No repercussions: *You're absolutely right. You've done an excellent job and I should have come to you sooner about this. I'm only sorry that, along with your promotion to deputy manager, I can't offer you a salary increase right now. However that's something we can review again in the coming months. Congratulations.*

When & bonus? I understand this isn't a decision that's made in a vacuum. Can you give me a commitment to review the matter again in four months? And I'd like you to consider that a one-time cash bonus could serve as a noncontroversial reward for the contributions I've already made.

the employee back to look for any ways to pursue the opportunity that would cost less, or for places where cuts can be made to free up funds for this new effort.

It's a more serious matter when an employee comes to you to say there's an impending disaster that can only be averted with an injection of funds. This isn't something you can ignore or hand off to them for further thought. Instead, you need to ask them to put together all the information and projections they have on the matter, bring it back to you as soon as possible, and then sit down with you at a subsequent meeting at which the two of you can go over the issue together and come up with a plan of action. If sufficient funds aren't available to put the resulting plan into action, you'll need to bring the matter to your own manager's attention. See Workscript 5.5.

Whether it's to take advantage of an unforeseen opportunity or to ward off an inevitable disaster, asking for an increased budget is an inherently political act. You are staking a claim for more funds than the company has allocated, requiring them to be taken away from some other division, diverted from some other use, taken out of reserves, or borrowed. You're also raising a red flag that, if unheeded, could have severe repercussions for not only you and your immediate boss, but the company as well. Doing this at a time when money is tight is even more fraught with peril.

The best way to handle this request is to come in already prepared with answers to whatever questions you might be asked ... in writing. You want to have memos that document, not only your findings and your ideas, but your fruitless efforts to look for alternatives. These memos aren't just working outlines and memory aids. They are proof that you raised these issues to this person, on this date. In effect, they are levers that shift the burden of responsibility for a negative outcome toward your manager, and away from yourself.

In the final analysis, this may not be your decision to make. Your goal is to make sure you receive the credit of discovery, but not the blame for failure.

The best time to have this meeting is as soon as you have gathered together all the information. If you can approach your manager spontaneously before business hours, that's great. Otherwise, make an appointment for as soon as you can, as early in the day as you can, providing the most time possible for discussion, decisions, and actions.

If you're unable to convince your manager to take the action or bring the matter even further up the ladder, your only alternative is to also offer a calendar that outlines exactly what steps you'll have to take when the disaster hits and exactly when you'll have to take them, providing advance warning and opportunities for the company to prepare for the inevitable events. See Workscript 5.6.

Requests for Time Off

If someone working for you needs a day off to deal with a family emergency, or a health issue, and has used up all their sick or personal days, don't treat it as a major issue. Simply ask them to make up the time later. If they need extended time off to deal with a similarly vital human issue—say a death in the family—the situation is more problematic.

Asking an employee to immediately use their vacation time for time off for an unforeseen family emergency may make financial and procedural sense, but doing so will come with a heavy cost. Making a bereaved employee use some of his or her vacation time to bury a dead spouse is the kind of response that's going to spread along the grapevine faster than a viral video spreads through the Internet. Every employee, and every employee's family and friends, will soon think of you as

Workscript 5.5 Responding to a budget increase request

An idea: *I know money is very tight now, but I've discovered what could be a golden opportunity for us. One of our competitors has been hit with a supply problem and the major customers in his home region are facing a desperate shortage. If we could increase our sales expenditures and expand our delivery network, we have a real chance to expand our market share overall and make inroads into a new market.*

Trouble ahead: *I just got word that our suppliers in the Northeast market have suffered a major hit. We're not going to be able to fill our orders. We're going to need to budget some emergency funds and quickly line up replacement suppliers or else we'll lose our customers to one of our competitors.*

No money: Thank you for bringing this idea to me. It's just the kind of quick thinking and insight that we want from all our employees. While your idea has a great deal of merit, there simply aren't sufficient extra funds available to take advantage of this opportunity. But please keep up the good work.

Alternatives: That is an excellent idea. It's great that you're looking out for these opportunities for the company. Unfortunately there's no money available to pursue this right now. I'd like you to come back to me in the next couple of days with a memo outlining alternative ways we could try to take advantage, either without spending more, or by taking money from someplace else in the budget.

I'll go upstairs: Thank you for coming to me with this idea. It's just the kind of initiative we want from our employees. Even though money is tight, I think it's worth pursuing. As a fall-back plan, I'd like you to come up with a memo outlining ways we could do this without added funds, even if it means cutting elsewhere. Meanwhile, I'm going to go upstairs and see if we can get the money.

Great job: Great work spotting this ahead of time. We need to work together to do everything we can to forestall this. Go back to your office and put all the data and projections you have together and bring them back here for a planning session this afternoon at 3 o'clock. After we come up with a plan, I'll bring it upstairs and present it to upper management.

Workscript 5.6 Requesting a budget increase

An opportunity: I've discovered what could be a golden opportunity for us. One of our competitors has been hit with a supply problem and the major customers in his home region are facing a desperate shortage. I know how tight money is right now, but if we could increase our sales budget by 10 percent for the next two months and expand our delivery network for that same period, we'd have a real chance to expand our market share overall and make inroads into a new market. I've explored all the alternative methods for possibly taking advantage of this opportunity without increasing the budget, and have scoured existing expenditures for places where we could cut back, but I haven't found any way to take advantage of this other than increasing the budget. Here's a comprehensive memo outlining the opportunity, my failed efforts at finding noncash options, a breakdown of what it will cost, and the potential gains.

Trouble ahead: I just got word that our suppliers in the Northeast market have suffered a major hit. We're not going to be able to fill our orders. We're going to need to budget some emergency funds and quickly line up replacement suppliers or else we'll lose our customers to one of our competitors. I've prepared a memo outlining the situation, providing an abstract of all the data and projections, and describing as well all my fruitless efforts to come up with alternatives to increasing the budget. I think we need to act quickly to forestall problems.

Great job: *Great work spotting this ahead of time. You have my approval to spend the sums you've requested. I'll send word down to finance and have my assistant prepare a memo formalizing my approval. Good work.*

No money: *Thank you for bringing this to my attention. I appreciate the import of what you've said and the work that went into your presentation, but there simply aren't sufficient funds available to increase the budget right now.*

I'll go upstairs: *Thank you for coming to me with this and doing such a good job outlining the situation in your memo. I'm going to go upstairs and see if we can get the money.*

Disaster dates: In that case, here's another memo that could be helpful. In it, I've listed all the dates when we'll have to take certain actions if there's no increase in the budget. If nothing else, this can give the company a chance to prepare responses for the inevitable results.

Workscript 5.7 Responding to a request for time off

Death in the family: *My father just died and I'm going to need some time off work to arrange the funeral and clean up his affairs.*

Nonemergency issue: *I've decided to have stomach stapling surgery. I've been desperately trying to get an appointment with a specialist and I've just learned he can fit me in next Monday, so I'll need to take the week off.*

Condolences: I know I speak for all of us in the company in offering my deepest sympathies and heartfelt condolences. Don't worry about things here. Please take a week off to take care of yourself and your family. If there's anything else we can do, please let us know.

Okay, but: While I would have liked more notice, I think we can overcome your absence for the week. I'll speak with bookkeeping and let them know you'll be taking one of your vacation weeks starting next Monday. I hope the surgery goes smoothly.

ONE WEEK LATER

Need more time: *Thank you for all your support in this trying time. I haven't been able to tie up all the loose ends of my late father's estate, so I'll need to take more time off.*

Okay, but: I understand. I'll let bookkeeping know that you'll be taking another week off and I'll have them arrange for your vacation pay to be applied to the time so you're not docked.

a heartless company. Word will leak out to vendors, suppliers, and customers as well. And eventually potential employees will learn that your organization is cold-hearted and uncaring.

I believe that if an employee asks for a week off to deal with a legitimate personal emergency that was unforeseen and beyond their control, you and your company need to put humanity (and morale) over money, bite the financial bullet, and give him or her a week off with pay that doesn't reduce their vacation time. Of course, if the request is for time off for something flippant or which could have been foreseen, there's no reason you shouldn't insist on vacation time being used. You should also subtly make clear that you're providing *one* week off with pay. If the employee comes back and asks for more time off, no one—inside or outside the company—would quibble with your telling them that it must come out of their vacation time. See Workscript 5.7.

Chapter 6

MANAGING UP

For decades, career-conscious middle managers have been encouraged to "manage" their relationships with their own supervisors with as much, or perhaps even more, care than they gave to managing employees. The idea was that you should do whatever you could, within propriety and proper protocol, to stand out from the crowd. The goal was prominence; to become, literally, the most outstanding among equals.

Today, it's the tallest daisy that gets cut first. Achieve too much prominence and you can become a threat to your boss. Stand out from the crowd and you make yourself a target, not only for backstabbers and fearful supervisors, but for bean counters and cost cutters as well. All employment is fleeting, so it's better to stay off the radar than to become too visible.

The idea now is to strive for success, not prominence. Do your job well and make your boss look good. Let him or her become prominent, if that's what they want. They can become the face for your superior results. Be the number-one producer who only attracts attention when the latest sales figures are released. The place you want to shine is on the spreadsheet, not the golf course. Keeping your head down and getting results are the best ways to make yourself valuable and nonthreatening to your boss.

The first area in which you can apply this approach is in talking to your boss about problematic projects. Work project issues are perhaps the most common of all those covered in this book. But that doesn't make them either routine or simple. Projects are, after all, the essence of what our jobs are all about. We largely base our perceptions of our employees on the way they deal with the projects we've assigned them. And our own employers base their perceptions of us on how we deal with the projects we've been assigned. Most projects become routine for those whose job it is to work on them. It's the rare problematic projects that take on disproportionate importance in how our performance will be judged and how we judge the performance of others.

Turning Down an Assignment

Avoiding a negative judgment is very difficult if you decide you need to turn down an assignment. This can be a no-win situation: say it's a bad idea and you could insult your manager, who may have been the person who came up with the idea; say you don't have the time and your manager could think you're lazy; and if you say you don't have the skill for the project your manager could lower his or her estimation of your abilities.

I suggest that you never refuse a project by citing that you think it's a bad idea. You haven't been asked for your opinion on the project; you've been charged with enacting it. Questioning its wisdom puts you in the worst possible light: you're not simply "refusing orders," you're exceeding your authority or responsibility in a way that your manager could feel is threatening. Instead, you need to either argue that you're not the right person for the job, or that you've got too much on your plate already.

Don't say you can't do a job. Instead, say you believe there's someone in the company who could do it better. Have a specific person in mind and cite a particular skill or ability. Similarly, don't say you don't have the time to tackle a job. Instead, say you need your manager's help in setting priorities for you since you're already working on so many other projects.

If your manager accepts your refusal, do your best to repair any self-inflicted damage by subtly emphasizing everything you are doing and will continue to be doing. If your manager insists on your taking this project on, don't continue to resist. Try to dilute the responsibility and workload somewhat by suggesting the formation of a committee or group to focus on the project.

The best time to have this discussion is early in the day, early in the workweek. If you can speak with your manager prior to normal business hours, that's best of all, since it will afford you undivided attention. (See Workscript 6.1.)

If one of your employees refuses a project you've assigned them, don't waste time trying to change their minds. Whether your employee's reasons are sound or not doesn't matter. The fact that he or she has decided to risk alienating you in this way, at a time when job security is nonexistent, proves they won't be able to do a good job. Consider any alternatives they suggest, but keep in mind these suggestions might be motivated by politics. There's no point engaging in criticism. Just thank the employee for being so honest. However, weigh their refusal and what you feel were their true motivations the next time you judge and rate their job performance.

Workscript 6.1 Turning down an assignment

On second thought: I've been reviewing that project we discussed last week. I can understand why you're excited it, but after thinking about it, I realize I may not be the best person for the job.

Plate too full: While I'd love to take this job on, I'm already devoting all of whatever extra time I can find to putting together the annual report, which you'd made a top priority.

There's someone better: While I think I'm the firm's best marketer, I think this project really needs our best salesperson, and that is Jane Jones.

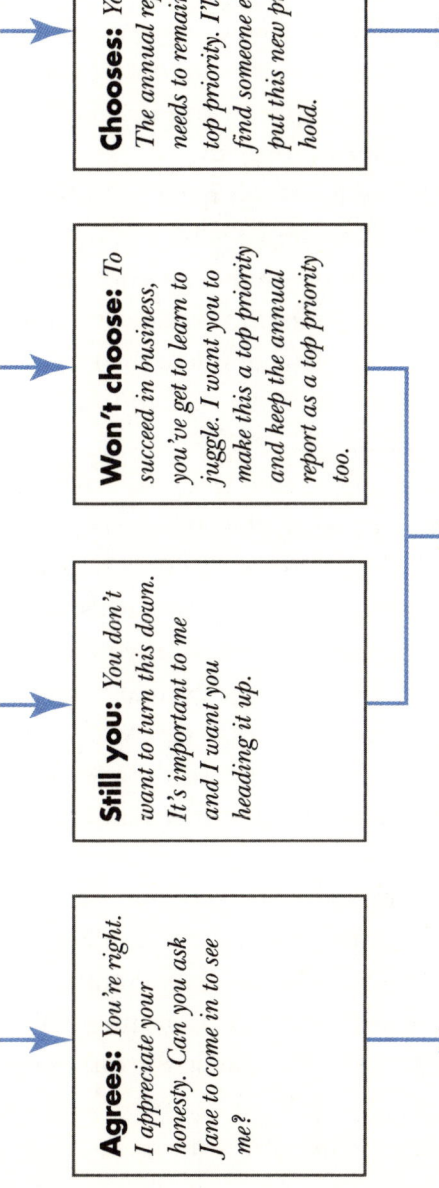

Asking for Relief from a Project

Trying to get released from a project which you've already commenced is riskier than refusing to take the assignment in the first place. That's because it can be perceived that you're admitting defeat. Unless handled adeptly, it can dramatically alter how you're perceived within the company.

The only way to minimize the potential harm is to frame this as an objective problem for the company. It's not that you don't have the time, it's that your department can't deliver the kind of quality job the company deserves in the time available. It's not that you don't have the ability to complete the task, it's that your department doesn't have the skills needed to deliver the kind of work the company expects.

Since any kind of change in midstream will result in some cost to the company, you need to stress that the costs of not making the change would actually be greater. Deflect personal attacks by affirming that you're putting the company's interests above your own. Prepare a memo outlining your argument, which you can present to your manager, but also which, more importantly, you can keep in your files in case you're not given relief and your fears are realized. That won't free you of some responsibility, but it will force your direct manager to share in any fallout.

Don't pursue this effort unless you're certain that the alternative—that is, staying with the project—will result in disaster. Your reputation and status will take at least a temporary hit from this, whether or not you succeed in getting relief. Your goal is to do your best to keep the damage from being permanent.

There's no good time to have this conversation. Don't delay or procrastinate. The sooner you have this dialogue, the sooner you'll recover from any damage. See Workscript 6.2.

If you're approached by an employee who wants relief from an active project or assignment, your only judgment should be who can replace them and how the change will be managed. In the current work environment, when someone comes to you and says they can't do the job, they're trying to avoid disaster, not maneuver politically. Relieve them, consider their suggestions about replacements, but make your own independent assessment.

Asking for a Deadline Extension

The secret to asking for a deadline extension is to make it clear that your only problem is time; nothing else is wrong. Rather than coming to your manager with an apology and a series of reasons for why you're not going to be able to meet the established deadline, steer the conversation as quickly as possible to the solutions. The past is past, the future result is still to be determined.

The mistakes were made in the original setting of the schedule, not in efforts made subsequently. Either the scope of the project or the difficulties were not fully understood early on. Now that the actual dimensions and elements of the project are clear, you can come up with a realistic, achievable deadline. Whatever the response, steer the conversation to your plan, which you'll deliver in writing as well as verbally.

There are always three general options available when deadlines are unachievable: get more time, hire more help, or submit a partial result on the date with the final product to follow later. Your plan should explore all three options but make the case for one in particular.

Have this conversation as soon as you realize you won't be able to meet the deadline. Procrastination will only make the situation worse and make you look less professional. See Workscript 6.3.

Workscript 6.2 Asking for relief from a project

Reengineering needed: I think we need to do some minor reengineering and I need to run the situation by you.

Lack skills: For the past year, my department has been handling municipal credit analysis as well as our usual corporate credit analysis. According to the projections I just received from the home office, the bank's municipal business is going to rise 300 percent in the coming year. We won't be able to handle that volume effectively. I think we need to form a separate municipal group.

Project problem: I've done an analysis of the Jackson project and I'm worried we're not going to be able to meet their timetable. As much as I'd like to keep the assignment, I think the best way to insure a timely delivery is to pass the project along to Jane Jones's group. I've spoken with her and her team would be able to better fit the Jackson project into their schedule.

Status Quo: *Your group has been doing a good job so far. Besides, setting up a separate group could be costly for the company.*

Don't disappoint me: *I picked you and your team for a reason. I hate to bring new bodies in at this stage. I'm counting on you. Don't disappoint me.*

Potential liability: We've been able to do such a good job so far because the volume has been light. We just don't have the skills or the functional ability to handle the kind of volume they're projecting. While a new group might carry costs, I think they're less than the risk of potential liability.

Don't want to: That's exactly why I'm suggesting this change. We don't want to disappoint you or the client. I'm afraid that the only way you could meet their timetable is through a reduction in quality, which no one wants.

Workscript 6.3 Asking for a deadline extension

No can do: We need to talk about the Jackson project. There's no way it can be completed in the 30 days we have available. I need your help in coming up with a solution.

Calm but curious: *What went wrong?*

Nervous: *Time is of the essence. We've committed to completion by that date.*

Angry: *I should have known I should have run this project myself rather than rely on you to deliver.*

Disappointed: *I relied on you. This is a real disappointment.*

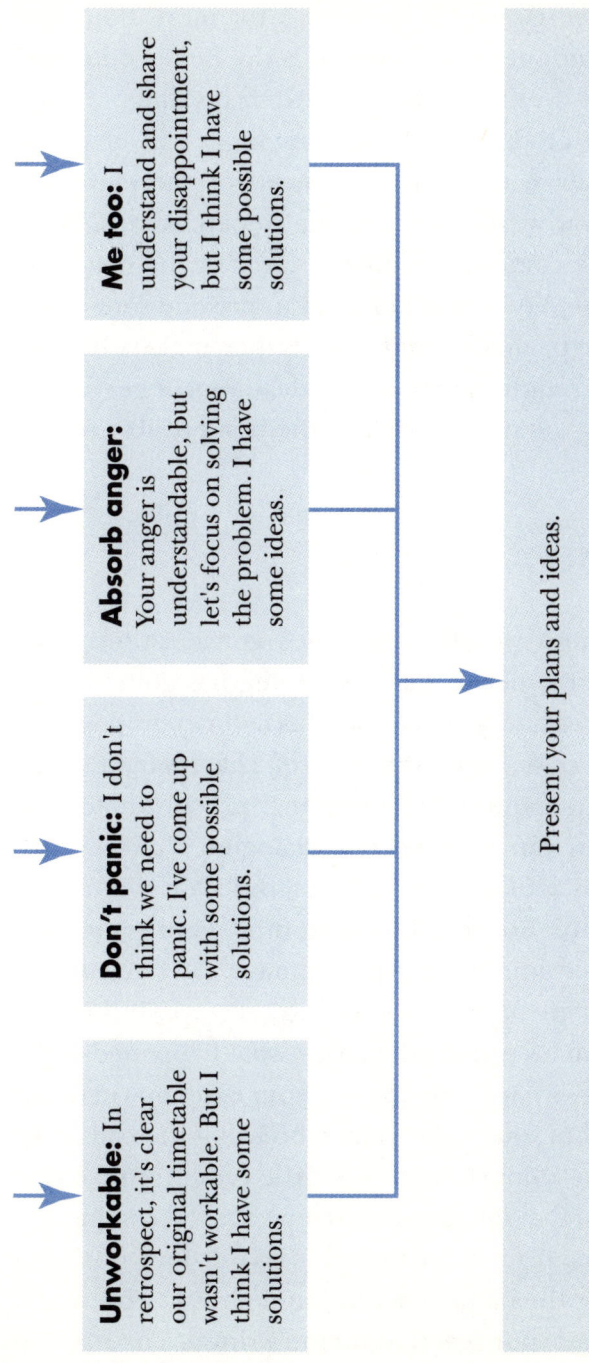

If an employee comes to you to ask for more time, you need to make a judgment as to which is the better outcome: lower quality, but on time; more costly, but on time; or high quality, but late. In today's workplace you have to assume that the deadline really is impossible to meet for the employee to have risked your wrath and potential repercussions. What you need to do is come down fully in favor of the deadline, the cost, or the quality. You don't want to provide something that's both lower in quality and late. Either make whatever compromises are required to meet the deadline, or get fully as much time as you will need to deliver the best possible result.

Breaking Bad News

There are few more fearful workplace conversations than having to tell your superior that something has gone wrong. You're embarrassed and worried that this failure could impact your current job status and your future. That's why it's only natural, and quite common, to postpone, procrastinate, and do everything you can to avoid this dialogue. However, this normal reaction is actually the worst response you can have.

Your goal in this conversation is to fulfill your obligation of disclosure while minimizing the damage to your current and future employment. The best way to accomplish this is to turn the discussion away from the past—what happened—and toward the future—what do we do now? Your best hope of doing this is to ensure that you're the person breaking the bad news. That gives you the opportunity to put the event into context and present a plan that mitigates the damage to the company.

There's no need to burst into the boardroom during a meeting to deliver the bad news, but you do need to present it as soon as you have your reaction memo written. The need to be the one who breaks this news is more pressing than picking the right day of the week or time of the day.

If you bear some responsibility, own up to it immediately, and then pivot by taking responsibility for the reparation action as well. If the problem was beyond your control, point that out, but demonstrate that you are now back in control by presenting your planned response. Obviously, both of these tactics require you to have developed a plan prior to the meeting. Put it in writing so there's something tangible and positive for you and your superiors to focus on.

Absorb any anger or threats, realizing such feelings may be as much or more about the situation itself than about you. Keep doing whatever you can to steer the conversation toward solutions. See Workscript 6.4.

Warning your manager about potential rather than actual problems requires a careful balancing act. You need to provide as much advance warning as possible, but at the same time you need to have done sufficient investigation and preparation so the conversations go as well as possible. Wait too long and you appear as if you're not on top of the business. Send up the red flag too soon, and you can be perceived as the company Chicken Little. Give a warning without having a plan in place, and it looks like you're panicking. Craft too extensive a response plan, and it could seem like you've concealed the problem for some time. The key is to take just enough time to ensure there's evidence that your suspicions are more than just intuition, and then just enough time to come up with the outline of a plan.

Warning of Potential Client or Customer Problems

Be cautious when delivering the news of a potential client or customer problem. The fear is that your manager will react poorly and "blame the messenger." The best way to avoid that

Workscript 6.4 Breaking bad news to your boss

We've got trouble: I have some bad news. Although I think we'll be okay in the long run, Jane from Acme just called to tell me they're moving to the L&H Agency. She said it had nothing to do with our work, it was a dollars-and-cents move. [or] She had raised some concerns about our approach, but I was addressing them. They just jumped the gun on me.

Calm: *They're one of our biggest accounts. They've been with us for five years. What happened?*

Disbelief: *They've been with us for five years. Now they walk out with no warning and you think your handling of the account had nothing to do with it?*

Angry: *I can't believe you screwed this up. Do you know what this is going to cost us?*

Threatening: *If I can't count on you to handle Acme maybe I can't count on you to handle Apex either.*

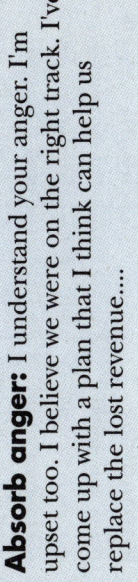

Absorb anger: I understand your anger. I'm upset too. I believe we were on the right track. I've come up with a plan that I think can help us replace the lost revenue....

Take charge: I think the economy was the straw that broke the camel's back. I've come up with a plan that I think can help us replace the lost revenue....

Workscript 6.5 Warning of potential client or customer problems

I sense trouble: Thanks for meeting with me on such short notice. I sense that Acme might be planning to pull its business from us. No one has said anything but my intuition is telling me something is wrong. I think we should arrange for the two of us to preemptively meet with the owners of Acme to potentially forestall any problems.

Angry: *What did your team do? Acme is vital to our business. If we lose them, heads will roll.*

Panics: *If we lose Acme we're in trouble. The head office will be out for blood. What are we going to do?*

Paranoid: *I think you might just be paranoid. If they haven't said anything, let's not rock the boat.*

Calm: *Can you tell me what you're basing this feeling on? If we can identify the problem, we can fix it.*

Redirect: I think the problem is at Acme, not with us. We need to find out what their problem is. That's why I'm suggesting we set up a meeting with them as soon as possible.

Soothe: If we react quickly we can avoid the problem. That's why I'm suggesting we set up a meeting with them as soon as possible.

Cautious: I think it would be a mistake to ignore things. Even if there's nothing wrong, it can't hurt to just sit down with them and show we care.

Explain: It's nothing specific. Just a feeling based on a change in their tone on the telephone. Let's meet with them and see if they identify a problem.

Workscript 6.6 Warning of potential vendor or supplier problems

I sense trouble: I think we might have a future problem with Service Corp. I just heard through the grapevine that they've signed on to supply our major competitor, who potentially could provide Service Corp. with greater volume.

Confrontation: I think we should confront Service Corp. with our fears and see if we can get some kind of commitment or renegotiate with them.

Internal change: I think that if we shift to shipping from the end of the week to the beginning of the week, we could get a jump on our competitors and guarantee we won't get short shrift.

Alternatives: I've come up with an alternative vendor for us, but suggest we sit tight for now and see if my fears are borne out.

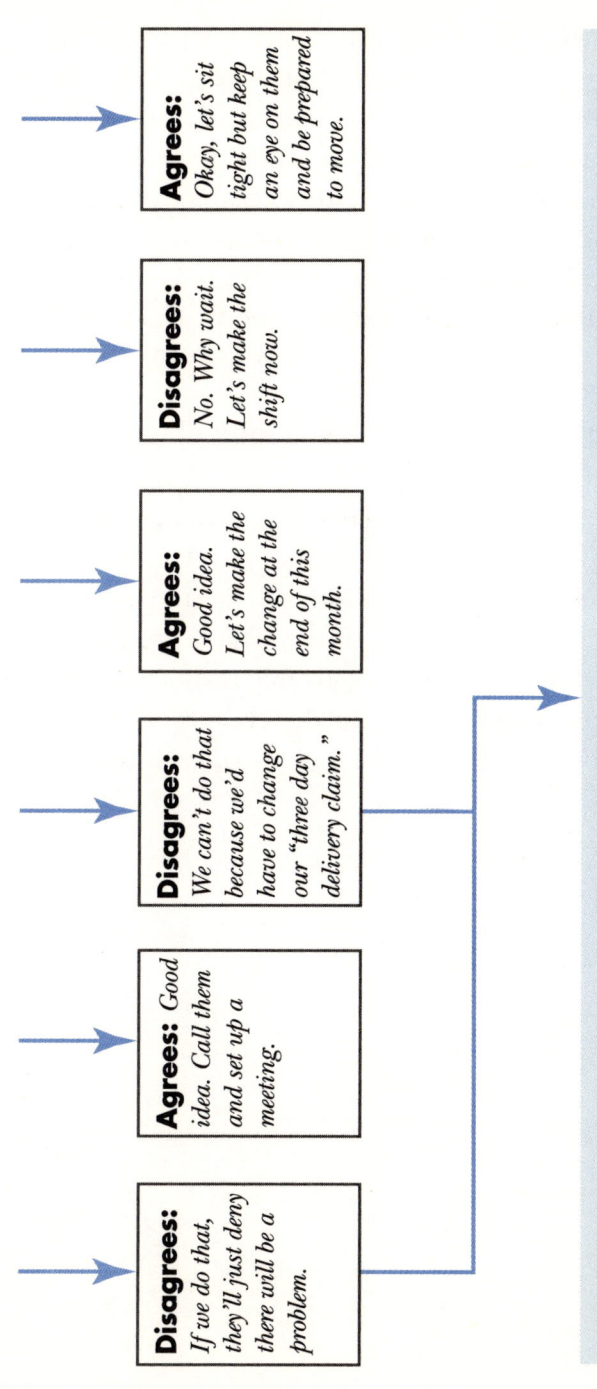

is to assume as much control over the conversation as possible. Give your manager a chance to vent, but steer the discussion toward your possible solution and away from the causes. There will be a time for a postmortem, but now is the time for action. If you can subtly show that you're not to blame, that's fine, but don't veer toward pointing a finger. The more you can get your manager involved as part of the solution, the more he or she will focus on the future, not the past. See Workscript 6.5.

Warning of Potential Vendor or Supplier Problems

You'll have more room for preemptive action in dealing with potential vendor or supplier problems than you'll have in dealing with possible client issues. While you still want to bring this to your manager's attention as soon as possible, you should spend a bit more time planning out possible responses. That's because it may make sense to act immediately, rather than wait for your fears to be proven accurate. See Workscript 6.6.

Chapter 7

GETTING PERSONAL

The current workplace environment, in which there's no trust, no security, and in which face-to-face communication is rare, has resulted in a toxic tone for workplace conversations about personal issues. Relationships are so antagonistic that most are viewing every personal interaction as either a potential weapon or a possible shield.

Employees, realizing that their jobs are in danger, are understandably willing to take advantage of any grounds they might seize on to claim unfair treatment. Employers, realizing that today they can fire almost with impunity, are using veiled and subtle hints to force changes in behavior or attitude.

As a manager, you need to weigh every word you use in a conversation about personal issues as if you were stepping into a minefield . . . because you are. Preparation and scripting for these situations is more important than ever before. You have a great deal of power to influence employees with just the subtlest act or word. But one misstatement could provide the employee with all the opening needed to threaten legal action.

And just to make the issue more pressing, in today's workplace you need to speak and act with the speed of light. You need more preparation than ever, but you have less time than ever to prepare, whether it's for dealing with office gossip, flirtatiousness, or slovenly dress.

Appearance Improvements

There's a reason some companies insist on uniforms for their personnel. Appearances matter to every organization. Clients and customers are greatly influenced by the appearance of those with whom they interact. Consciously or not, the public will equate their perception of an employee with their perception of an organization. A disheveled salesperson sends the message that the company is unorganized.

Even if employees never interact with clients or customers, their appearance is important. That's because proper garb has an internal function as well. Dressing professionally says to coworkers that you take yourself and your job seriously. If you don't care how you look, you probably won't care about how you perform.

Many managers assume that employees will choose proper attire on their own, either through prior experience or by observing how their peers dress. Unfortunately, you can't rely on everyone getting the message unaided. Some employees, intentionally or unintentionally, may choose to make their own unique fashion statements, which can undermine the image you're trying to convey.

If one of your employees isn't dressing appropriately, you need to intervene directly. If your company has written instructions for dress, get a copy that you can hand over during your conversation. Be direct and clear. Stress that this is a question of appropriateness, not taste or style. If you fear that a conversation with the employee might stray into controversial gender-related areas, have another person of the employee's sex present. Your mantra should be professional, not personal.

Have this conversation the first time you personally observe inappropriate dress. If you let it go even once, you're condoning fashions that could become contagious. See Workscript 7.1.

Appearance includes more than just clothing. Poor hygiene can be even more problematic, with customers and coworkers. Such problems are almost certain to undermine the image of the company if the offending employee comes in contact with clients. Hygiene problems will erode his standing in the company and will block any future progress in the organization.

Having to tell someone their breath or body odor is offensive may be one of the most awkward situations you'll ever face in the workplace. Yet sometimes it's essential that you take action, not only for the comfort of you and other coworkers, but for the company and the person's future as well. Begin with the assumption that he or she isn't conscious of the problem. Start off by subtly suggesting the same tool(s) you use to avoid similar problems. If he or she takes the hint, let the matter drop. If your subtext isn't understood, you'll have to press further.

Try not to be embarrassed. They will be embarrassed enough for both of you. Remember: You are doing this for their own good. Do this immediately after lunch and in private, and if you're using any props, such as breath mints, make sure you have them on hand. See Workscript 7.2.

Workscript 7.1 Asking employees to improve their appearance

Establish authority: I need to talk to you about something that might make you uncomfortable. Part of my job is ensuring our staff looks and acts in a professional manner. Your attire today is not appropriate professionally.

Disheveled: You look as if you slept in that outfit. And it's stained. You look disheveled.

Informal: You're wearing a sweatshirt and jeans. You look as if you are going to the mall, not to work.

Provocative: I'm shocked by the way you're dressed. A tube top and miniskirt are not appropriate for the office.

Excuse: I usually dress well. I was in a terrible rush this morning and I just threw this on.

Personal: How I dress is my personal business. It's not your business.

Angry: You're the only one who has complained. Maybe you shouldn't be looking.

154

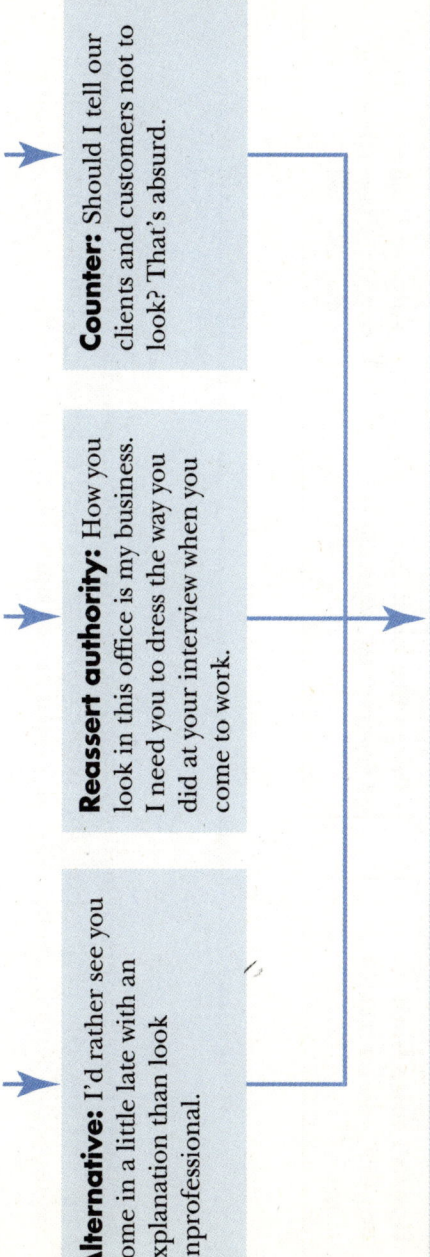

Alternative: I'd rather see you come in a little late with an explanation than look unprofessional.

Reassert authority: How you look in this office is my business. I need you to dress the way you did at your interview when you come to work.

Counter: Should I tell our clients and customers not to look? That's absurd.

Fix it: If you come in with inappropriate attire again I will send you home, on your time, to change. And if it happens after that your job will be in danger.

Workscript 7.2 Asking employees to improve their hygiene

Bad breath: [Show mints, pop one in your mouth.] Would you like one? I don't know about you, but sometimes I really need one of these after lunch.

Body odor: You won't believe the sale I stumbled on. The drugstore up the street was offering 50 percent off on antiperspirants and deodorants. You should check it out.

Doesn't take hint: *No thanks. I never use those kind of things.*

Takes the hint: *Um . . . sure. I appreciate the suggestion.*

Angry: *Excuse me. Are you suggesting there's something wrong with me?*

Be direct: There are some things even your best friend is too embarrassed to tell you, but you should know. You have a discernible body [or] breath odor, and you need to address it. I'm bringing this up because it could cause problems for you in your career and for the company with clients and customers.

End Backstabbing

Backstabbing peers will always rationalize their behavior by claiming they're just offering constructive criticism or that they have only the company's interests at heart. That's why it's essential you respond by pointing out that the comments are actually both unfair and personal. While these confrontations can be uncomfortable, you shouldn't feel defensive or uneasy. You're coming from a position of honesty and are simply looking for justice.

Overt attacks require direct responses. But covert attacks are best dealt with through indirection. That prevents the backstabber from simply denying involvement and effectively ending the dialogue.

If the incident is done in public it requires an immediate public response, followed by a private conversation. If it is not a public attack, approach the backstabber privately as soon after the incident as possible.

Have this conversation in the other party's office. Show up unannounced and unscheduled. If you're using an indirect approach, sit down as if for a friendly chat. If you're directly challenging the other person, stay on your feet, between them and the doorway, forcing them to listen to you. Then, when you finish, turn your back and leave. See Workscripts 7.3 and 7.4.

Dealing with backstabbing among your employees is actually more difficult than addressing the backstabber when you're the subject of the attack. That's because the secrets to dealing with this situation are investigation and verification. If you haven't witnessed the backstabbing firsthand, you must verify it. It's not uncommon for an employee to try to manipulate management into punishing an office enemy by accusing them of backstabbing. Verifying a complaint means interviewing all the affected workers, including the alleged perpetrator.

Workscript 7.3 Publicly putting an end to staff backstabbing

Indirect private approach

Indirect approach: I've heard that someone has been complaining that I'm not pulling my weight. What do you think I should do?

Rationalizes: The same thing happened to me last month. This place is getting so political, don't you think?

Appeal for unity: I agree, and it's really not good for anyone. We'd all make more money if we worked together, or at least if we didn't stab each other in the back.

Confrontational: What do you expect? We all want to be promoted but there's only one opening, so it's every man or woman for him or herself.

Threat: That's not the way to go. If these things don't stop, I'm going to suggest to the boss that we have a department-wide meeting to air our feelings openly.

Denial: I can't believe someone would do that. Maybe you misunderstood a comment that was meant to be helpful?

Appeal for privacy: If that was the case, I'd have hoped the person would come to me directly and privately with the suggestion.

Quite often the investigation is enough to bring the problem to a halt: word spreads that you're aware of the problem, consider it serious, and are ready to deal with it accordingly.

The unease workers feel criticizing peers to management is part of the shield protecting the abusive subordinate. You must be prepared to penetrate this wall of silence. Employees should be told they're not being singled out but are among many being interviewed. Emphasize that all responses are strictly confidential. Solicit feedback about the problem in general without attaching a name to initial queries. However, once initiated, the interview should call upon specific incidents, and you must press for the identification of a specific individual. Collective anonymity can provide a cover that encourages honest responses. It will also add considerable weight to the meeting with the actual backstabber.

Once you're comfortable with the facts, move quickly. Call the employee into your office. Stay behind your desk, seated. Be straightforward and specific. Deal with the problem as an existing one, not a suspected one. Review what the problem is, how you verified it, and what you'll do about it. Don't engage in debate. Say you have the verification and want the problem to stop. Conclude the meeting by citing what specific action you will take if there are further occurrences of the problem. See Workscript 7.5.

Halting Sexual Harassment

If you're being sexually harassed, you must deal with the situation immediately, despite the fear and discomfort. The longer this kind of treatment is allowed to go unanswered, the more frequent and aggressive it will become. The key to putting an end to it is to deliver a powerful, unequivocal, even

Workscript 7.4 Privately putting an end to staff backstabbing

Direct public response/private approach

Public rebuke: I can't understand why you'd want to slander me this way in public. I suggest you stop this public display and we discuss any personal issues you have with me in private. But right now, I suggest we get back to work.

LATER THAT DAY

Express shock: What have I ever done to you to elicit this kind of behavior? I can't imagine why you're attacking me this way.

Rationalizes: *Last year someone told the boss my staff was demoralized. I know it was you. I'm just responding in kind.*

Confrontational: *Listen, we all want this promotion. If you can't take the competition maybe you ought to remove your name from consideration.*

Denial: *I didn't attack you. I just point out a couple of mistakes you've made lately in the hope they won't happen again.*

Appeal for unity: I've never attacked you—that's not my style. I like working with you, not against you. But if we can't work together, I'd appreciate your cutting out the attacks.

Threat: I'm all for a fair fight. I know what you're doing. If you keep it up, I'll suggest we sit down with the boss and discuss our problems openly.

Appeal for privacy: If you're really interested in helping me, come to me privately, don't bring things up at staff meetings. I'll do the same for you.

Workscript 7.5 Confronting someone who's backstabbing you

J'Accuse: We have a serious problem. One of our staff is constantly criticizing and demeaning the work of others behind their backs. It's at the point where morale and productivity are going downhill. I've done a thorough observation and have no doubt you are the person responsible for the turmoil.

Deflects: *I don't believe this. Everyone complains. I'm here every day and I do my job. Why are you singling me out?*

Validate: You've singled yourself out. A number of your coworkers, not just one, made it clear that you are the source of the problem. This behavior stops right here, right now. Any further incidents and your job will be in jeopardy.

Confirms role: *Sometimes I complain and bitch. But so does everyone else. I never meant any harm.*

Warn: Your comments appear to have gone well beyond just complaining. The behavior stops right here, right now. Any further incidents and your job will be in jeopardy.

Acceptance: *I understand. I was just blowing off steam. Maybe I got carried away. I didn't mean to hurt anyone. I was just joking around. It won't happen again.*

Make excuses: *This is unfair. I don't care what any of them said. They don't like me beacuse I don't socialize with them. I can't believe you'd let them do this to me.*

On notice: There's no excuse for your actions. You've placed your job in jeopardy and severely strained your relationships with your coworkers. Any such incidents in the future could cost you your job.

threatening objection. There should be no effort made at somehow measuring the response to meet the harassing acts or comments. An off-color joke has to be met with equal vehemence to a grope. Not only do you not want to be perceived as weak, you don't even want to be perceived as reasonable when it comes to this issue. This is as much about power as it is about sex. Your goal is to seize back the power. If that means you appear nasty, angry, or irrational, so be it. You want the other party to be afraid of you.

Go to the other party's workspace, position yourself between where they are sitting and the door, remain standing, maintain eye contact, and walk out as soon as you're done, ensuring you have the final word. If you anticipate any trouble, speak with someone in human resources prior to the meeting. See Workscript 7.6.

Surprisingly, it's easier to confront someone who's sexually harassing you personally than someone who's accused by a third party. That's because in the first instance you're certain of the facts and can have a one-on-one, person-to-person dialogue that transcends office hierarchy. On the other hand, when one employee complains to you about the actions of another, you can never be certain of the facts, and must be just as concerned about the rights of the accused as the rights of the accuser. That being said, it's vital you put an end to the harassment. The secret is to focus attention not on the actions or intent of the accused, but on the perceptions of the accuser. Facts are actually less important than putting your foot down hard so that this doesn't happen again.

Have this dialogue as soon as you're made aware of the situation. Any delay will fan the accuser's anger. Call the accused into your office and stress that the conversation is private and confidential, but potentially devastating to future employment. See Workscript 7.7.

Covering Up and Ratting Out

When a peer asks you to cover for them in some way, chances are it's to avoid getting in hot water for something he or she did—or didn't—do. Since you don't want to get a reputation as a liar or appear to be a partner in crime, your goal should be to make clear that you won't lie, without coming off as condescending or holier-than-thou. You're walking a tightrope between maintaining good relations with your coworker and your employer. If this is the first time the coworker has asked for your "help," you can lean a little to his or her side of the tightrope. If this is clearly an habitual problem, lean toward your manager's side. But if this incident falls somewhere between unique and habitual, you'll have to try to strike a balance. See Workscript 7.8.

There are times in everyone's work life when you get fed up covering for a peer's failure to perform or incompetence. But deciding to complain to management about these failings is a big step. Even if your complaints are accurate and in the company's interests, you can be labeled a backstabber and alienate not only your peers but your manager, too. That's why the only time you should "rat" on a peer is when their poor performance or procrastination is threatening your ability to get the job done, and you've tried unsuccessfully on your own to set things right.

At that point it's worth going to your manager and asking for direct intervention. You need to show remorse at having to take this step, but determination that what matters most is the success of the company. Give some careful thought to the timing of this conversation. You want to wait long enough so that the manager's intervention is necessary, but not so long that even this intervention might not be enough. See Workscript 7.9.

Workscript 7.6 Confronting a sexual harasser

Grab attention: I want you to stop working and listen very closely to what I'm about to say. Your behavior toward me is totally unacceptable and must stop right now.

Overreacting: *Relax. You're overreacting. It was just a joke. You're taking this too seriously. Why don't you cool down and we'll just forget about this?*

He said, She said: *Oooh, I love it when you get mad. Seriously babe, it's your word against mine. So why don't you forget about it and come to lunch with me?*

Untouchable: *You don't scare me. I can make your life here miserable and destroy your future in the industry. Nothing will happen to me.*

Apologetic: *I'm sorry. I didn't mean anything by it. I was just joking and never meant to offend you. Can't we just forget all about this?*

166

→ **Not a game:** This is my profession. Ours is a business relationship. Period. I come here to work, not play games.

→ **On record:** I thought you might respond this way. That's why I spoke with personnel before coming here. They told me to try to speak with you before filing a formal complaint.

→ **Threat:** That's not what my attorney says. And I don't think that's what they'll say upstairs after my attorney speaks with them.

→ **On notice:** I hear your apology. Still, there's no excuse for that behavior. I've prepared a memo outlining the whole situation but will hold onto it for now.

Workscript 7.7 Ending staff sexual harassment

Serious problem: Jane came to me recently and told me about your conduct. She regards it as harassment. Regardless of what you had in mind, this is an extremely serious problem that threatens you and your career, as well as the company. We must nip this problem in the bud.

Denies behavior: *Listen, I don't know what she's talking about. I didn't do or say anything to her that was in the least sexual.*

Blames victim: *Hey, you know what she's like. She's got no sense of humor. She's a real prude. I was just joking around.*

Can't understand: *I can't imagine what I could have said or done that would make her feel that I was harassing her. I feel terrible.*

Perception: What you did or didn't do isn't the issue here. What matters is her perception. You've got to take care of this situation.

You have a problem: I don't know if Jane has a problem or not. But clearly you have a problem now. You've got to take care of this situation.

Doesn't matter: In a situation like this, your intent doesn't matter. All that matters is her perception of your words or actions. We have to address her complaint promptly.

Marching orders: You are not to have any personal interaction with Jane, and you're to keep your business interaction with her to the absolute minimum required to get your job done. You are to have a third party present whenever you meet with her. I will convey your apologies to her. I don't want to have to speak to you about this kind of situation ever again.

Workscript 7.8 Refusing to cover up for a peer

Lie for me: *I need your help. You know that obnoxious rep from Acme who I just lost my temper with? Well, she said she's going to complain that I was rude to her. If you're asked about what happened, could you tell the people upstairs that she's full of it?*

Habitual behavior: No way. You've been warned about this kind of behavior before. The people upstairs aren't stupid. They'll know I'm covering for you. I know she's a pain, but you need to apologize to the rep right now and then immediately go upstairs yourself and tell them what happened. That way you can show them you've got a handle on things and are working to improve your temper.

Pattern developing: If I'm asked, I'll explain that the rep is a nightmare to work with. But you're losing your temper way too much. You've got to get a handle on your behavior because the rest of us aren't going to be able to cover for you. This is going to get you into serious trouble if you don't put a stop to it.

First time: If I'm asked, I'll definitely explain how difficult this rep can be and what a hard time she was giving you. I won't lie about your response, but I won't bring it up, and if asked, I'll explain it's the first time I've ever seen you lose your temper with a sales rep.

Blocking Brownnosing

The employee who sings your praises no matter what you do is actually undermining your credibility and authority. The public nature of extravagant flattery can add embarrassment to the mix. The longer you let such brownnosing go on, the more you risk having others believe this is the behavior you value and will reward. An employee who thinks you'll be impressed by transparent praise and unsought personal attention is insulting your integrity and should make you angry.

Confront the "suck-up" as soon as your instincts tell you that you're being targeted with excessive compliments. The best time is immediately following an incident. Expect an initial response of shock and surprise to your efforts. Next will come pleas of innocence. You might even receive more excessive praise. The key is emphasizing that it is the perception of the actions and comments that is destructive, regardless of the intent. See Workscript 7.10.

Finishing Flirtations

An overly friendly employee, who is often touching or violating your personal space, and who regularly includes double-entendres in his or her dialogues with you, represents one of the most difficult challenges you're likely to face as a manager. Feeling flattered is a natural reaction, but you need to not only maintain your objectivity, but demonstrate that objectivity to this employee and the rest of the staff. This isn't acceptable workplace behavior.

The best way to deal with a flirtatious employee is to document and establish the behavior. Keep a record of incidents and ask your peers if they've noticed the behavior. Then,

Workscript 7.9 Ratting out a peer

Reveal: I'm afraid there's a problem with meeting our deadline for the Oxford proposal [or] I'm afraid the Oxford proposal may not be up to our usual standards. I've asked several times but Sean has yet to turn in the final sketches for the project [or] The sketches I've received from Sean just aren't up to par.

Upset at ratting: That project is crucial. I made you the lead person on it and I don't want to hear any excuses or buck passing. Your job, and Sean's, is to get it done right, and done on time.

Reassure: I'm sure we'll get it done right and on time if we solve this problem right now. But to do that I really need your help. Without it, I don't think I can get what I need from Sean.

Willing to listen: *I'm not going to let anything get in the way of us delivering on this project as promised and on time. What exactly is the problem?*

No delivery: I know Sean is under a lot of pressure, as are all of us. But I'm not sure the sketches have even been started. I've asked for them repeatedly and gotten no response.

Poor quality: I know Sean is under a lot of pressure, as are all of us. But the sketches I've gotten just aren't of the quality we need. We've spoken about it repeatedly, but there's been no improvement.

Time running out: We're running out of time, so to make sure we deliver as promised, I need you to intervene on my behalf with Sean.

Workscript 7.10 Putting an end to brownnosing

Angry: I'm angry and annoyed with you. I've had enough of your fawning and flattery. It's over the top and embarrassing. It has to stop.

Denial: *I haven't done anything. [or] You can't be serious. How can you even think that?*

Examples: You personally deliver my mail, you bring me donuts, you praise me in meetings. It is embarrassing.

Deflects: *I don't understand. You're upset because I happen to be kind and considerate? And what's wrong with giving credit where it's due?*

Focus: What's wrong is that it comes off as calculating and transparent. It is embarrassing.

Rationalizes: *I'd think you would be pleased that I respect what you say and feel free to say so. I certainly don't feel embarrassed.*

Clarify: Obviously not. But I want it to stop. If others think that all I value is being flattered, no one will take me seriously.

Future outcome: This will be the last time we talk about this. Let's move on. If you can't, I will call you on any further brownnosing on the spot. I won't care who's present.

call the employee into your office. Remain seated behind your desk, objectively cite your observations, explain that the behavior is adversely affecting you and the organization, and insist that it come to an end.

Don't be surprised if you're accused of wishful thinking or sexual harassment of your own. Refuse to be rattled or to go on the defensive. Avoid comments or issues that could steer the conversation in a personal direction. This is less about getting agreement than it is about asserting your perception and the reasons for it. See Workscript 7.11.

If the flirtatiousness comes from a peer it's potentially less problematic, unless of course you're not interested and it escalates into your receiving a social invitation. It's important not to react with anything other than seriousness. Your goal here is to deflect the unwanted attention while maintaining a civil working relationship. Unfortunately, this might not be possible.

The simplest method is to say you admire the individual as a coworker but you're not interested in developing a personal relationship. Most people will accept the rejection. Some will persist in either asking for a reason or by continuing their wooing. Since continued unwanted wooing can only lead to a discussion about harassment, I think it's best to provide a reason. Of course, you still need to be diplomatic.

You can explain that you don't mix your business and personal lives. If that's true, the problem is solved. But if it's clearly untrue, or if it becomes untrue later on, you risk alienating your admirer. He or she may or may not accept that your statement was a diplomatic opportunity for them to save face.

Another option is to explain that you're already involved in a serious relationship. Once again, if true, the problem is solved. But if your admirer somehow learns your relationship is a fiction, he or she could become annoyed.

Workscript 7.11 Stopping a flirtatious employee

Uncomfortable: An office works best when everyone feels comfortable, and I haven't felt comfortable lately. I'm afraid my discomfort has to do with you. I feel your behavior toward me in the workplace, often in the presence of others, can only be described as flirting.

Surprised: *Flirting? Me? What are you talking about?*

Detail: I'm talking about the conversations where your hand is always on my arm or shoulder, going out of your way to brush against me, your constant compliments, and your frequent off-color insinuations. I've been keeping a record of the kind of behavior I described, just to make sure I'm being totally professional and objective.

Shift responsibility: *I don't believe what I just heard. I think you're seeing what you want to see.*

Authenticate: It's not just me. Others have commented about your behavior to me. And I've been keeping a record of the kind of behavior I described, just to make sure I'm being totally professional and objective.

176

Discomfort: *A record! My God! I feel like some kind of criminal! It's so embarrassing!*

Counters: *Is what people think important as long as our jobs get done? Isn't that the most important thing?*

Share discomfort: I've felt embarrassed as well . . . in front of my entire staff.

Refute: Your behavior is making me feel uncomfortable and has been observed by others in the company.

Threaten action: This behavior has to stop right now. If it doesn't, I'll need to speak with human resources.

The bottom line here is that when you turn down a social invitation from a peer who is somewhat persistent, you must accept the risk that the working relationship with this person can become difficult. See Workscript 7.12.

Silencing Gossiping

Gossip is routine in most workplaces. But its ubiquity doesn't make it any less divisive. Unrelenting, focused attacks on a single worker create fear, resentment, and apprehension in all workers. The gossipmonger is rarely called to task by colleagues, and is often protected by the silent shield of everyone's penchant to gossip. The result is the undermining of the equilibrium and effectiveness of the workforce. This script's goal is put an end to the pronouncements of your office gossip. Your willingness to acknowledge the problem, consider it seriously, and confront the source are the secrets to success.

It can be extremely difficult to uncover exactly who is the source of the gossip in question, but rather than try to engage in an exhaustive investigation, go with your intuition and gut instincts and bring in all the potential gossips for individual conversations. Do this as quickly as possible to keep the contagion from spreading. Instead of focusing on this particular instance, describe gossip in general as the problem. Strongly state how professionally destructive and personally repulsive you find the behavior. Express your anger and annoyance at the situation, without pointing any fingers. Then, ask for the individual's help in solving the problem. See Workscript 7.13.

If you find yourself the subject of gossip, your instinct might be to lash out at the person you think responsible. Don't do it. You could be making a false accusation, the confrontation could damage your working relationship, and the

Workscript 7.12 Stopping a flirtatious peer

Asks for date: *Would you like to go out to dinner and a movie with me this Friday night?*

No: I'm flattered that you asked, but no thank you.

Not interested: I admire you as a coworker, but I'm not interested in taking our relationship any further.

Involved: I'm already involved in a serious relationship.

No mixing: I insist on keeping my personal and professional lives completely separate.

Wants explanation: *Do you mind if I ask why?*

Workscript 7.13 Putting an end to staff gossiping

We have a problem: We have a serious problem in the office with gossip. It's apparently becoming personal and hurtful.

Some evidence: I couldn't help overhearing you holding court by the coffee machine this morning. I know everyone gossips, and I'm not saying you're responsible for the hurtful personal attacks I've learned of, but I wasn't pleased by what I heard earlier.

No evidence: I've gotten reports from a number of people that someone is spreading malicious rumors about the personal life of one of the secretaries. Have you heard anything about this?

Denies responsibility: *I'm sorry about that. I didn't mean anything by it. Even though I might have spoken out of turn this morning, I'm not the gossip you're looking for.*

Stonewalls: *'Gossip isn't anything new or uncommon. But still, I haven't heard about any particularly malicious personal attacks.*

Enlist help: I'm glad to hear that. Since you're well connected with the rest of the staff, I'd really appreciate your help in solving this problem. Could you spread the word that I'm concerned about this and that I consider personal attacks and gossip to be completely unacceptable? Let everyone know that, whatever the intent, this kind of innuendo is hurtful and unprofessional and will not be tolerated.

accusation could lead the person to spread even more malicious stories. Instead, engage in some subtle indirection. Treat the other party as your ally, not your enemy. Explain the damage the gossip is causing and then enlist their help in stamping it out. Try to have this conversation just after lunch, and have it in your "ally's" office or cubicle. See Workscript 7.14.

Drying Out Drinking

In large organizations there are official policies for dealing with employee drug and alcohol problems and perhaps even individuals on staff trained in bringing such issues up with employees. But most small companies have no formal procedures or resources for these troubling matters. Instead, it often falls to a manager. If you're eager to retain the individual, you're going to need to impress on him or her the need to rehabilitate, or at the very least to clean up his or her act during working hours.

Hold this difficult conversation as soon as possible after an incident in which the problem was obvious. Call the employee into your office and explain that it's entirely private and confidential. Be as businesslike as possible, stressing that you're concerned with job performance, not personal behavior. You're not interested in the reasons for the behavior, only that it is affecting work and must stop.

Expect anger, denial, and projection, but reiterate that this is a workplace problem that needs to be addressed. Then, keep your fingers crossed that the shock therapy works. See Workscript 7.15.

It's more difficult having this conversation with a peer. Even though his or her excessive drinking may have an impact on your ability to do your job, you have very little leverage. The problem is compounded when the drinking is taking place at a sales conference or some other quasisocial setting. There's little you can do at the moment without creating a scene; and

Workscript 7.14 Confronting a gossip

Upset: I'm very upset. Someone is going around the office spreading the rumor that I'm dating Sean. Can you believe that?

Plays dumb: *That's terrible. Do you have any idea who it could be?*

Confronts: *Well, that's true, isn't it?*

Play along: No, but I wish they'd stop. It's bound to make them, as well as me, look unprofessional.

Irrelevant: The point isn't whether or not we're dating, it's that my personal life is no one's business but my own.

Ask for help: If you find out who it is who's spreading these rumors, I'd really appreciate it if you would tell them to stop, not just for my sake, but for their own.

Workscript 7.15 Confronting an employee with a drinking problem

Warning: I called you in here to tell you that your job performance is not as good as it should be, and I think the reason is your drinking at lunch. You're not here to maintain potential. You're here to realize it.

Denial: I don't know what you're talking about.

Job's fault: This is an awfully stressful job. It's not like I'm coming in drunk after lunch.

Still best: Even after a couple of drinks at lunch I'm still the best salesman you've got.

Angry: You have no right to say that to me. My personal life is my business.

No debate: I don't want to get into a debate with you. Something is effecting your performance and whatever it is needs to stop. When I hired you I looked forward to a long relationship. I still want that... if possible.

Less pressure?: When I hired you I saw someone who could handle pressure. No amount of drinking is going to make this job easier. If you want me to take some of the pressure off you, that can be arranged.

Need your best: You're right. You do your job well. But you're even better when you don't have a couple of drinks in you. The company, and you, need to be the best you can be.

You're right, but: You're right. Your personal life is none of my business. But this is affecting your work and that is my business. It could end up affecting how you earn your money.

Get it together: We're having this conversation because I don't want to fire you. I want you to succeed. We have a problem here. I need you to address it. I'll help if I can, but it must be addressed.

185

Workscript 7.16 Confronting a peer with a drinking problem

Affecting work: I need to speak with you about something that's affecting the way we work together. I think you need to stop drinking when we're working together. It's hurting our chances to close deals. Drinking gives clients an excuse to drink more and lets them avoid making decisions. And to be honest, sometimes you're not careful about what you're saying.

Myob: My drinking is my business. It's not like I'm getting drunk on the job. What I do outside the office is none of your business.

Exaggerating: I don't drink that much. I think you're exaggerating. Maybe I got a little buzzed when we were out with the people from Acme, but so did they.

Jealous: Listen, just because you have a hard time letting your hair down and don't know how to have a good time with clients doesn't mean I've got a drinking problem.

Works for me: I know it's not your style, but socializing with clients works for me. I think the people from Acme had a great time last night.

Wrong: You're wrong. Your drinking in business situations affects the company and my livelihood.

I wish: I wish I were exaggerating, but I'm not the only person who has noticed it. You really should tone it down.

Working: I resent your implications. But when it comes to business I'm more concerned with closing the deal than having a good time. I think you should be too.

No sale: It may have looked that way, but here we are the next day without a signed contract. We didn't do any business last night.

My stake: I'm not the boss, but I have a stake in the success of our working together. If your behavior continues to harm my ability to do my job, I will discuss it with the boss. The next time we meet Acme, let's try to do it in a nondrinking situation, like breakfast or an in-office meeting.

187

he or she may already be doing a good job of that. Instead, your goal should be to try to keep it from happening again. All you can do is ask him or her to tone it down, at least when you're part of the picture.

Have this conversation as soon after an incident as possible. Be direct, clear, and determined. You're doing this for your peer's long-term interests as well as the company's and your own. Expect denials or counteraccusations, but keep the focus on the behavior. Compassion is fine, but what matters most is that his or her problem stops affecting your career. See Workscript 7.16.

Ending Internet Privilege Abuse

For almost a century companies have been concerned with employee pilferage. Full-blown embezzlement and theft was always very rare, but the petty theft of office supplies and other incidentals was so common as to become just another cost of doing business. In today's information age there's a more pressing concern than missing paper clips. Abuse of Internet privileges can result not only in wasted money, but worse, in wasted time. And if this wasn't a sufficient cause for concern, there's the potential for problematic or illegal activities, such as browsing porn or downloading pirated files, on the company's equipment. Many employees today consider personal Internet use while at work to be just one more benefit. It's up to you to keep this activity within acceptable limits so that the issue doesn't come to the attention of your own manager.

The essential element of this dialogue is preparation. Gather, from firsthand observation and electronic tracking, evidence that there's excessive personal use. Make it clear that activity which has come to your attention can also come to the attention of others, and that it needs to be reined in. See Workscript 7.17.

Workscript 7.17 Putting an end to Internet abuse

Capture attention: I'm concerned with a problem I've observed over the past couple of months. You seem perfectly at ease using the company's Internet access for your own personal use. [Pointing to reports on desk.] If it were only an occasional e-mail or web visit, it wouldn't be an issue, but these logs show that you're spending a considerable amount of time using your Internet access for personal use. This is costing the company money and has to stop now.

Singled out: *Everyone does some personal things online during the day. Why are you singling me out?*

Own fault: It's the facts that have singled you out. According to the logs you are the biggest abuser of Internet privileges in this department. I'll be speaking to others as well, but what you need to focus on is your behavior. It must change. Now.

Not a big deal: *I make a great deal of money for the company. Sending the occasional e-mail and browsing online now and then isn't that big a deal. It's not like I'm not doing my job.*

Bottom line: Your successes have brought you to the company's attention, but so too can your failings. Abusing your privileges to this degree is costing the company money and eventually that will come to the attention of the people upstairs. This has to stop now.

Workscript 7.18 Questioning an employee's expenses

I have a problem: I went over your recent expense report and I have a problem with it.

Too much: I'm glad you took the people from Acme out to dinner. The bill for dinner was $600 for four people. That's just too much.

Personal expense: You've included the cost of an in-room movie on your hotel bill. The company doesn't reimburse you for entertainment that isn't business-related.

Blameless: I made the mistake of letting them pick the restaurant. If it had been my choice, I would have picked someplace else.

Pushback: I realize it's a lot of money, but they're big clients. In the long run, don't you think it's a good investment?

Protests: I worked 18-hour days on that trip and I didn't think an in-room movie was that big a deal. It's not a lot of money.

Apologizes: I'm sorry. I completely forgot about it. It won't happen again.

Explain: I'm glad you took them to dinner. Next time make sure you take control of the situation and choose the restaurant.

Explain: It's fine that you took them to dinner. They are important clients. However, you don't need to take them to such an expensive place to demonstrate that we appreciate their business.

Not cost: It's not the cost that's the issue. It's a matter of judgment. The company isn't responsible for your personal entertainment, whether it's $10 or $100.

Ease fears: I understand. That's what I thought had happened. We all make mistakes. That's why I check the reports over.

Deflating Expenses

Questioning an employee's expense report should be an educational opportunity rather than an inquisition. The amounts in dispute are probably quite small, so there's no reason to turn this meeting into a back-and-forth of accusation and denial. Chastising someone for wanting reimbursement for a personal expense of a few dollars will do nothing other than alienate them. And overly criticizing an employee for spending too much on a justifiable expense could lead them to overreact in the future.

Your goal is to make the employee aware of an error in judgment, if they've spent too much, or to explain to them what spending is appropriately personal, rather than a reimbursable business expense. Never assume malicious intent. If the employee wanted to steal from the company, it would be surreptitious and not involve an obvious line on an expense report. Hold your temper even if you get a little pushback. It's probably defensiveness born of fear. Use this as a teaching moment.

There's no good or bad time to have this conversation; hold it whenever convenient. Assume the manner of a mentor and advisor rather than a disciplinarian. It's okay to crack a knowing smile or two. See Workscript 7.18.

If your own expense report is questioned, you need to provide an explanation for what you can only characterize as an error or omission. Either you didn't exert sufficient control over a situation, and as a result the clients forced you to spend too much, or you didn't sufficiently vet the expense report to edit out a personal expense. You can subtly set the stage for this by immediately assuming there's a problem of documentation, the most common error of omission in an expense

Workscript 7.19 Defending your own expense report

Announces problem: I brought you in here to discuss your recent expense report. I have a problem with it.

Puzzled concern: Is there something wrong with my documentation?

Spent too much: *Your documentation is fine. The problem is that you spent $600 for a dinner for four. That's way too much money.*

Not my choice: You're right. I made the mistake of leaving the choice of restaurants up to them. And since they're such good clients I didn't feel like I could turn them down. It won't happen again.

Personal, not business: *Your documentation is fine. The problem is that you've got about $100 here for in-room movies. That's not a business expense.*

A mistake: I'm sorry. I didn't realize that was on the report. I used the rapid check-out and didn't have a chance to audit the bill before submitting it. I'll take care of it right away.

report. By agreeing that the expense was too high, or apologizing for mistakenly seeking reimbursement of a personal expense, you show your employer you're not in need of further education. It was a mistake, which you're aware of, and which will never happen again. See Workscript 7.19.

Chapter 8

LOOKING OUT FOR NUMBER ONE

For years, career experts, myself included, would stress that if you helped your company, you helped yourself; that those who contributed to the company's bottom line would be seen as assets and would be valued. But, sad to say, that has changed. Today, everyone from the man sitting in a basement cubicle making telephone sales calls, to the woman in the top-floor corner office who reports only to the board of directors, is a temporary employee. The only rational response to this situation is to look out for number one.

You need to approach performance reviews, networking meetings, job interviews, giving notice, and negotiating salary with laserlike focus on your own needs, not those of the other party. It pains me to say it, but concessions or offers you make out of anything other than mercenary motives will not yield a similar response in kind. Today, when you turn the other cheek in the workplace, you just get slapped twice.

That doesn't mean you're free to be overtly self-centered. However much everyone intellectually understands the situation, it's not yet politic to acknowledge it. Even a nod-and-a-wink approach could get you branded as not being a "team player." And while that's a trait that earns no rewards in the modern workplace, the perceived lack of it can result in your being branded.

The solution is to rationalize your actions as results of the workplace environment, and to describe your motivations as being for personally pure motives. It may look like you're trying to extort a termination agreement, for instance, but you're just doing it to protect your young and growing children. In other words, try to demonstrate that your ends justify your means.

Performance Reviews

For generations of employees, performance reviews were annual rituals to be anticipated with either fear or excitement, and sometimes both. Held near the anniversary of initial employment, or during an assigned departmentwide period, these employee/manager dialogues focused on past performance, future development, and current salary.

For the successful employee, the annual review was a chance to make the case for a pay raise, to get a pat on the back for past efforts, and to be given developmental marching orders for the coming year. For the struggling employee, the annual review was a time when prior difficulties would be painfully enumerated and benchmarks for improvement would be set, but also a moment at which promises of turnaround could be made. For the employee whose past year was a mixed bag, some successes and some failures, the review was an opportunity to emphasize the former and rationalize the latter in an effort to set the stage for a fully positive next year.

In general, reviews used to be all about the employee. In today's workplace environment the nature of annual reviews has been turned on its head. Now, they are all about the manager.

With salary increases as rare as four-leaf clovers, even the most successful employees can't realistically expect an annual review to result in a raise. At a time when employees simply don't trust their employers, it's very difficult for the two parties to engage in the kind of open and honest discussion that could actually empower, encourage, or correct. This situation is amplified because face-to-face communication is so rare. How can a manager list the ways an employee can secure his or her position when both parties know that no one, no matter how successful, is secure? How can a manager lay out a development plan for an employee who knows his or her job could be extinct in a year? How can a manager legitimately discuss the evolution of skills and responsibilities at a time when short-term results are all that matter? The answer, unfortunately, is that most managers today can't try to do any of this. Instead, they need to use the annual performance review as an opportunity to protect themselves.

The opportunity for a termination to become problematic is higher today than ever before. That's for two reasons. First, changing social attitudes and new legislative and regulatory efforts have expanded the types of employees who have some form of protection from "unfair" termination. And second, with so many more employees being terminated these days, the opportunities for problems have increased.

In response, most managers need to use the annual review as a chance to plant seeds for future potential terminations. Any critique given at an annual review can serve as justification for a termination in the coming year. The employee who's fired just before becoming fully vested in a retirement plan will be less likely to consider protesting if, for example, 10 months before his or her teamwork was criticized.

The annual review is also now an opportunity for managers to use employees as tools to secure and improve their own positions. Employee goal-setting should now be done with an eye toward improving performance in areas that directly translate to the manager's image. Rather than a forum to provide long-term developmental guidance for the employee, it has become a tool to burnish management's short-term image.

This necessarily self-centered approach to annual reviews by managers needn't be completely unfair to employees. Some humanity can be added back into the process if, as a manager, you explain to the employee how the corrective or developmental steps you're suggesting can benefit the employee in the long run . . . even if that means at another place of business. By acknowledging the transitory nature of employment today, and encouraging steps that can help the employee in his next position, even if it's at another company, a manager will be as nurturing as possible in this workplace environment.

Astute employees can make the best out of a performance review today by similarly focusing on their own long-term development as individuals, rather than their progress as employees of their current company. Rather than asking for a raise, or providing defensive answers when asked for a self-critique, employees can volunteer an actual weakness, but one that can be remedied with the help of the company. Training and continuing education expenses come out of completely separate budget categories than salaries.

By acknowledging a flaw, employees provide managers with the future rationale they're seeking, in exchange for getting some company help in addressing that very flaw. While it's not the kind of win-win situation most of us would like, it's a far better outcome than coming away empty handed.

The scheduling of a performance review should be done by the manager. You don't want an employee to feel threatened, so give advance warning. Simply say that the anniversary of his or her hiring is coming up and you'd like to set up a time for the annual review that's mutually acceptable. If your own review date is looming and you haven't heard anything from your manager, don't stand on ceremony: take the initiative and launch the scheduling discussion yourself.

Many companies have specific procedures for conducting reviews, so by all means consult with human resources and follow your organization's rules. But even when the proceedings are somewhat orchestrated, it's important for you to prepare for the specific type of situation you're facing.

When, as a manager, you're reviewing an employee whose performance is average, you need to plant the seed for any future termination. Spend some time preparing for this meeting by gathering any documentation you can for the criticism you intend to deliver. Even if there are multiple issues, pick one to highlight. Otherwise the meeting comes off as a punishment rather than a review. Besides, if the employee is that bad, he or she shouldn't be working for you: fire them rather than review them.

If the employee accepts the criticism gracefully, respond with some encouragement, noting that if they follow your suggestions it can only help their security.

If the employee pushes back, employ the documentation you've gathered and explain, in clear terms, that continued employment depends on improvement. See Workscript 8.1.

If during your own review you're confronted with an obvious effort to plant the seeds for your future dismissal, resist the urge to debate the criticisms. Whether they're groundless or not, an argument will only make things worse. Instead, offer effusive assurance of your desire to make the changes requested. If before the review, you suspect you might be criticized for something in particular, make some independent efforts to preemptively address the "flaw." If, on the other hand,

Workscript 8.1 Delivering a critical performance review

Room for improvement: *You've been doing an acceptable job for the past year. However, in these days it's important for all of us to be more than just acceptable; we need to contribute to the company's success. After analyzing your performance, I think one thing you really need to focus on improving is your customer-service skills. I know clients [or] customers can be difficult, but you need to always remember that they are the ones that actually pay your salary. I'd like you to commit to doing better in the coming years.*

Accepts criticism: *I hear what you're saying and I will do my best to improve. I love working here and want to do the best job I can.*

Debates criticism: *I know I'm not the friendliest employee, but I don't think I'm as bad with clients [or] customers as you seem to believe.*

Encourage: *I'm glad to hear that. Improving your customer-service skills will go a long way to making your position more secure.*

Document: *I have a file with six different complaints from customers from the past year. I also have seen your impatience myself. You need to improve in order to secure your position.*

Workscript 8.2 Defending your own performance from criticism

Room for improvement: *You've been doing an acceptable job for the past year. However, in these days it's important for all of us to be more than just acceptable; we need to contribute to the company's success. After analyzing your performance, I think one thing you really need to focus on improving is your customer-service skills. I know clients [or] customers can be difficult, but you need to always remember that they are the ones that actually pay your salary. I'd like you to commit to doing better in the coming years.*

Prepared: I appreciate your insights. I'm aware this is a weakness of mine. In fact, I signed up for a course in customer service at the nearby community college. After just a couple of classes, I can already tell it's going to help me a great deal. I love my job here and want to do the best I possibly can for the company.

Blindsided: I appreciate your insights. I love my job here and want to do the best I possibly can for the company. I think there's a class in customer service at the local community college. I'll sign up for it tonight when I get home. I will do whatever it takes to keep my job here.

Encourage: *I'm glad to hear that. Improving your customer-service skills will go a long way to making your position more secure.*

201

you're blindsided by the criticism, do your best to come up with a spontaneous plan of action. The more specific you can be in describing how you'll address the criticism, the more secure your position will be. See Workscript 8.2.

When you need to review an employee who has done a good job, and who has no glaring weaknesses, your best approach is to ask the employee to engage in some constructive self-criticism. Not only will this potentially help spur improvement in an area of weakness of which you weren't aware, but it also provides you with the kind of information you'd need if you must terminate this person in the future.

If the employee voices an honest self-assessment, express your thanks and provide encouragement that working on this flaw can only help his or her position with the company. If the employee provides a backhanded self-criticism, which obviously isn't the subject of real self-assessment, call them on it. They've now given you the weakness to pinpoint. See Workscript 8.3.

If you're asked for self-criticism during your own review, you should use it as an opportunity to push for training in an area which you know will be of benefit to your long-term career, not just performance in your current job. Have a training or educational course in mind, and draft a memo outlining its advantages to the company and its costs. Present it to your reviewer, and ask that the company contribute to the cost of training. Whether your manager agrees, refuses, or is noncommittal, respond in the same way: Thank him or her for the support and for anything the company can do to help. See Workscript 8.4.

When you're reviewing an excellent employee, whom you'd like to retain if at all possible, planting the seeds for future termination isn't appropriate. Having done great work for the past year, the employee will be understandably frustrated if he or she receives only criticism at the review. Not receiving a raise, while disappointing, will be accepted as strictly a sign of the economic conditions. But not receiving praise will be seen as a punishment for hard work and effectiveness. Few things will send someone out on a job hunt faster than that. Instead, you need to give them some guidance about how they can improve their already good package of skills, making them not just a more valuable employee, but a more attractive employee for possible future employers as well. Your concern with their long-term development will go a long way toward compensating for the lack of increased pay, and to mitigating the atmosphere of distrust in the workplace.

If the employee tries to redirect your suggestion into a salary increase instead, gently resist the gambit. You can't blame them for trying. Instead, suggest that you may be able to get the company to pay for some or all of the training. Similarly, if the employee says that she or he can't afford the classes you suggest, offer to check with human resources to see if the company can foot the bill. See Workscript 8.5.

If during your own review your manager follows up high praise with the suggestion of some type of professional development program, resist the urge to use this as leverage to ask for a raise. Salary increases today are extremely rare, and when successful, are based not on past performance but on your pay not matching market value. Instead, thank him or her for their interest in your long-term development, and ask if the company can pay for or contribute to the cost of the program. Having suggested the course, your manager will be unable to say *no* right away and will have to check on your request. Once you've completed the program, whether or not the company contributed to its cost, it's likely that you will have jumped into a new category and will then not be receiving market value. You'll have an excellent argument for a raise and at the same time will have increased your value on the job market. See Workscript 8.6.

Workscript 8.3 Asking an employee for self-criticism

Self-criticism: You've done a good job for us this past year. I'm curious: Have you given any thought to areas where you think you need improvement?

Honest assessment: *Thank you. The only area I can really single out is keeping up with my record keeping. There are times when I let things pile up and then have to record them in one marathon session. I'm going to try to alter my work flow a bit this year so that I factor record keeping into my daily schedule.*

Dishonest assessment: *Thank you. I think that sometimes I let my workaholism get in the way of my relations with my coworkers. There are times when I feel they aren't working as hard as me, or taking the job as seriously, and I let them see my frustrations. I'll try not to let my dedication to the company get in the way of my teamwork.*

Encourage: I'm glad to hear you being so honest and self aware. That's just the kind of attitude that can help you become a stellar employee and make your position more secure.

Correct: Well, I don't think that's really a very analytic self-assessment. That's more a criticism of your coworkers than a self-assessment. I think you need to work on being more aware of your own weaknesses as well as strengths in the coming year. That will go a long way toward your becoming a stellar employee and make your position more secure.

Workscript 8.4 Responding to requests for self-criticism

Self-criticism: *You've done a good job for us this past year. I'm curious: Have you given any thought to areas where you think you need improvement?*

Honest assessment: Thank you. I've actually been thinking a lot about what could help me do my job better and be more productive for the company. An increasing number of our new clients are from Europe and I think that it would be of enormous benefit if we were able to communicate with them in their own languages. I don't know any foreign languages and I think that could be a weakness going forward. I'd like to take a class in business French that's being offered by the local college. Or perhaps order one of those language learning computer packages. I was hoping the company could help me with the cost of either the class or application. I think it would be an excellent investment for the company. I've prepared a memo that outlines the costs of each.

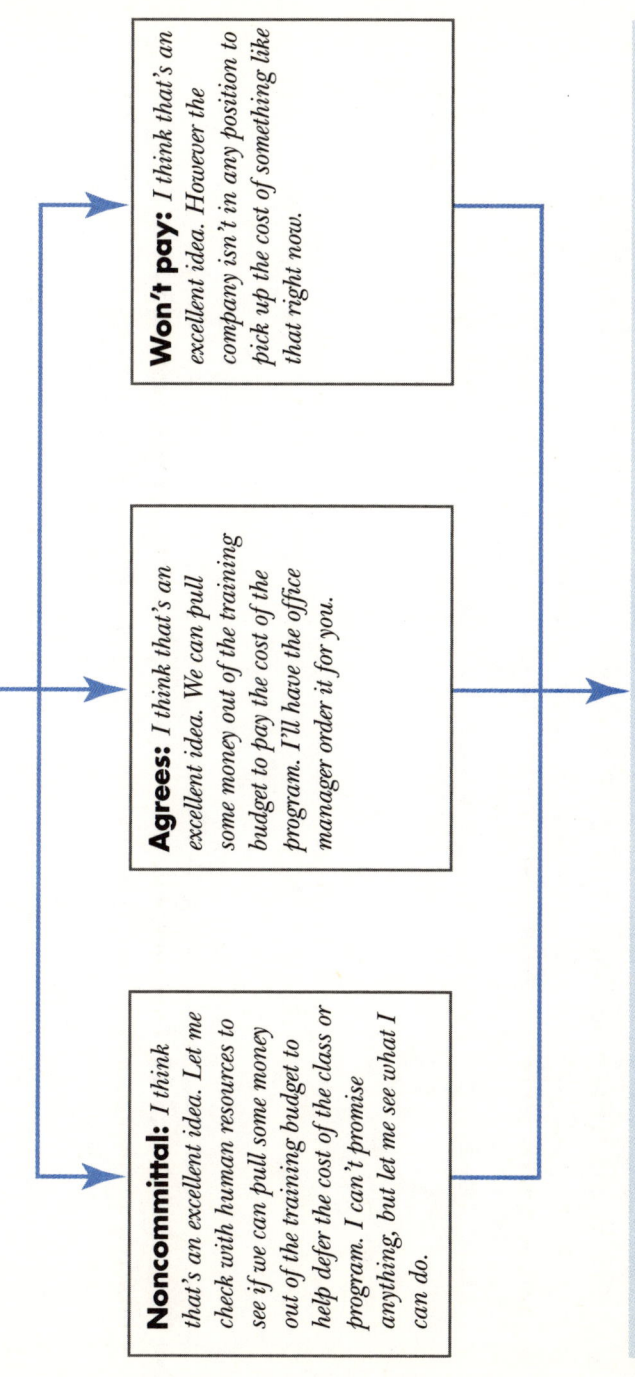

Workscript 8.5 Offering suggestions for professional development

Professional development: You've done an excellent job this past year. I'm very happy with your performance. I'd like to suggest something that could be beneficial, not just to your work for us, but for your long-term professional development. The one area where you're lacking experience and training is in information technology. I know there's a certificate program being offered at the local university. I think that knowledge will make you even more valuable to the company, and it's bound to help you down the road, too.

How about a raise? *Thank you for the vote of confidence and the suggestion. A salary increase would be an even more appreciated gesture. I think I've earned it.*

Thanks, but can't afford it: *Thank you for the vote of confidence and the suggestion. However, money is so tight right now that I don't think I can afford to pay for the program.*

Not possible: A raise simply isn't possible right now, not just for you, but for anyone. What I might be able to do is to get the company to pick up some of the cost of the IT program I mentioned. Let me speak to human resources and see if there's something in our training budget which I can pass along to you.

I'll check: I understand. What I might be able to do is get the company to pick up some or all of the cost. Let me speak to human resources and see if there's something in our training budget which we could use for you to take these classes.

Workscript 8.6 Responding to suggestions for professional development

Professional development: *You've done an excellent job this past year. I'm very happy with your performance. I'd like to suggest something that could be beneficial, not just to your work for us, but for your long-term professional development. The one area where you're lacking experience and training is in information technology. I know there's a certificate program being offered at the local university. I think that knowledge will make you even more valuable to the company, and it's bound to help you down the road, too.*

Can you pick up the cost? *Thank you for the vote of confidence and the suggestion. I think it's an excellent idea and I would be excited to learn more about IT. Will it be possible for the company to pick up some or all of the cost of the program? As you yourself have said, it would be an excellent investment for the company.*

I'll check: *Let me talk with human resources and see if there's enough in our training budget so we can either pick up the cost or at least contribute to the tuition. I'll get back to you.*

Renting a Contact List

Whatever the result of a performance review, in today's workplace you should be investigating potential opportunities all the time. I like to call this job fishing rather than job hunting. You need to have your bait, in this case your resume, constantly in the water, or job market, waiting to see what bites. That means networking should be part of your weekly schedule.

Professional networking web sites and organizations are fine for a number of things. They can provide a sense of community and let you know that you're not the only one feeling the way you do. You can get insights on how to manage the job fishing process, and maybe tips on some avenues you haven't pursued. Staying active in industry associations and organizations can provide ideas for potential approaches and ensure that you don't lose touch with important trends. The problem with these traditional approaches to networking is that most of the people you'll be networking with are in the same situation as you. Networking among other job seekers isn't likely to yield many leads.

Instead, I think you should be trying to get face-time with individuals who can provide you with insights, advice, guidance, and wisdom. You should be looking for those old standbys: informational interviews. Of course, many executives have sworn off these meetings, viewing them as nothing more than job hunts in disguise. But there is a way to get past this hesitation.

I'm a big believer in drawing on your social, rather than professional, capital when networking. I've come to believe that most jobs are filled because of personal, not business connections. A friend of the corporate president looking for a new marketing director, regularly golfs with an experienced marketing executive who's now out of work. The owner of a chain of coffee shops looking for a new manager goes to church with the wife of someone who has experience managing cafes and is always on the look-out for new opportunities.

It's these social connections that can result in networking interviews, which in turn can result in jobs. Renting someone else's contacts in this manner has a number of advantages. First, because it's an informal connection made outside the normal channels, you won't be part of a crowd. Second, personal connections are more apt to lead a busy executive who has sworn off "informational interviews" to go through with the meeting. It's much harder to turn down a personal request for a favor than it is a business request for a favor. Having some kind of personal connection, even if it's secondhand, provides you with leverage you can use to get face-time with someone who might otherwise balk.

Once you learn of a social connection to a potential networking opportunity, ask your firsthand contact to make the initial approach, in effect, prepping your target. While that's not a 100 percent guarantee you'll get the meeting you want, it increases your odds enormously.

You can also boost your odds by timing your call well. Most upper-level executives arrive early, get some of their own work done, and then spend the first hour or so of their day preparing their direct reports for the day's tasks. From, say, 11:30 A.M. until 2:00 P.M. they are planning for, traveling to, eating, or returning from lunch. Then from 3:00 P.M. onward, they're thinking about what loose ends need to be tied up by the end of the day. That gives you two narrow windows to make a call for an informational interview: from 10:00 A.M. to 11:30 A.M. and from 2:00 P.M. until 3:00 P.M. See Workscript 8.7.

Selling Your Career Shift to an Interviewer

Career and industry shifts are rapidly becoming the norm rather than the exception. Today, layoffs and terminations tend to be industry- and profession-wide rather than company-specific, resulting in a crowd of candidates pursuing the same shrinking number of openings. The solution is to shift either location, profession, or industry. Since so many of us have invested financially and emotionally in our communities, we're loath to move. That makes career changes more common than ever before.

While it might seem particularly daunting to interview in a strange business, remember that someone, somewhere in the organization believed your prior experience was applicable, otherwise you wouldn't have gotten the interview. That means this meeting is an opportunity to close the sale. You don't need to come in prepared to change minds, only to reinforce existing beliefs. Of course, you'll still be pushed. But think of these probing questions as chances to nail down an offer.

What you want to stress is that you'll have no learning curve. Remember, all that matters today is short-term results. You want to explain that you'll be productive from the moment you walk in the door. Training isn't needed. You have all the tools you need and you'll start using them on day one. See Workscript 8.8.

Negotiating Job Offers

I never thought I'd write this, but salary may not be the most important part of your negotiation if you're offered a new job. Raises, whether based on merit or tenure, are no longer automatic parts of the work environment. And neither are they always a good thing, since they could have the effect of putting a target on your back when it comes to the time when management must slash staff. Benefit packages aren't necessarily a vital negotiating area today either, since so many government programs have been created to take the place of employer-provided benefits.

Workscript 8.7 Asking for a networking meeting

Intro #1: Hello. Can I speak to Liz Walsh, please. It's [your name] calling.

Direct connect: *This is Liz Walsh.*

Gatekeeper: *Can you tell me what this is in reference to?*

Use name: Of course, Matt Gavin suggested I give Ms. Walsh a call.

Drop name: I'm glad I was able to reach you. Matt Gavin suggested I give you a call. I'm looking at making a career change and getting into the coffee bar business. Matt said you know that business better than anyone. I was hoping you'd be able to spare about 15 minutes to speak with me, just to share your thoughts on and insights into the industry.

Agrees: *Sure, any friend of Matt's is a friend of mine. Let me transfer you to my assistant and he'll set up a time with you.*

Leery: *Listen, I think Matt's great, but if what you're really doing is looking for a job I'd suggest you call human resources.*

Negative: *I don't know what Matt was thinking. He knows how busy I am. I'm afraid I can't help you.*

214

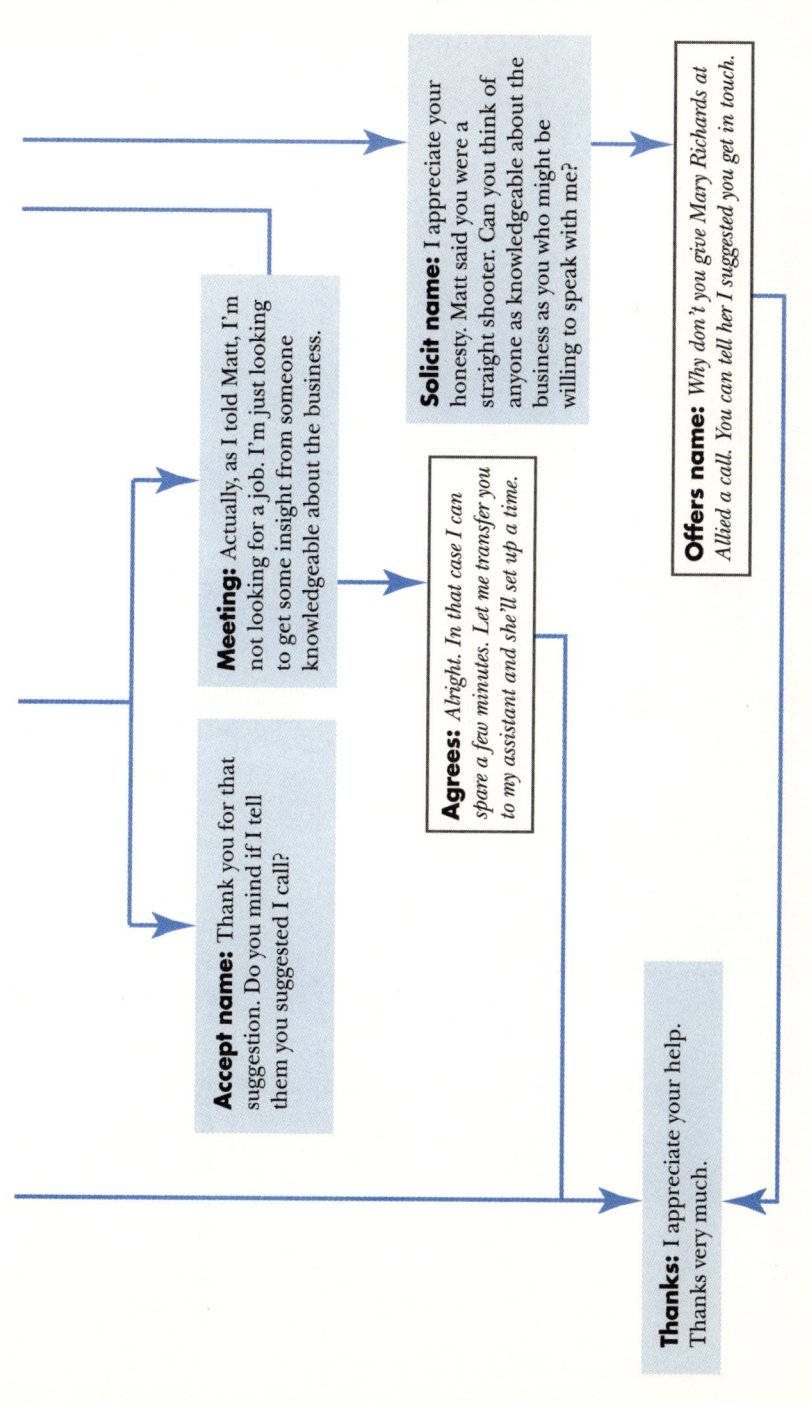

Workscript 8.8 Explaining a career shift to an interviewer

General probe: *What makes you think you're qualified to fill this position even though you have no experience in the industry?*

General counter: *While I've never been in your industry, I've solved the same kinds of problems, met the same kinds of deadlines, managed the same kinds of people, and done the same kinds of marketing. Even though I come from a different industry, I possess the same skills and abilities you require. For example [cite examples].*

Jargon/players probe: *That may be. But you're not familiar with the jargon we use, the language and culture of our industry [or] the players in the business, the people who make things happen.*

Jargon/players counter: *As a matter of fact, I've made a concerted effort to learn the industry's language [or] the players in the industry. I want to make sure this job isn't an experiment for either of us. From the day I walk in the door I'll be able to apply the skills, abilities, and knowledge I'll need to succeed. There will be a learning curve.*

Underlings probe: *I'm confident about your skills, but how will you deal with underlings who have more experience in the industry than you?*

Underlings counter: *I'll deal with them just as I've dealt with staffs in the past. I'll learn from them when I can and take their suggestions if valid. But I'll also demonstrate to them, as I have to you, that my experience and knowledge are transferable to this industry.*

Peers probe: *I'm afraid the other department managers may perceive you as a threat or as a sign that massive changes are coming. After all, someone with your background being named to this position would be unprecedented for this company.*

Peers counter: *I think fear of change is natural to everyone. I saw the same kind of problems in other industries. I've discovered that once people show they can do the job, all those fears vanish.*

Superiors probe: *You make a strong case for yourself. But you know, I may have a hard time selling you to the people upstairs. They're not as open-minded as I am.*

Superiors counter: *I understand. No matter how good an idea is, if it's new, it's tough to sell. Please let me know if there's anything I can do to help you with this. Also, please accept my gratitude for any efforts you can make on my behalf. No matter where I go in this industry I'll always be grateful.*

Workscript 8.9 Negotiating a job offer when you're still employed

Makes offer: *I'm very impressed with your qualifications and I think you're just the kind of person we're looking for. I'm offering you the position of department manager at a starting salary of $50,000. I know we're not the top paying company in the industry, but we are one of the healthiest. And with the economy being the way it is, that's the best we can do. What do you say?*

Market value: *I'm not obsessed with getting top dollar, however for me to leave I do need to know I'll be getting market value for my work. From what I've gathered, a salary of around $60,000 would be more appropriate for this position.*

Thrilled...but: *I'm thrilled at the possibility of coming to work for you. My sole remaining concern is my family's security. I'd be giving up a position at a company for which I'd worked for 16 years. If I was terminated there without cause, I'd qualify for a severance package equal to four months salary. What I'd like is a simple termination agreement that if I'm fired without cause, I'd receive that same severance package.*

Agrees: *I think that I can probably squeeze another $5,000 out of the budget. What do you say to an offer of $55,000?*

No more: *I know that we're not the top paying company in the business. But we can offer you things that others can't. I simply can't offer more than the $50,000.*

More than money: You're right that there's more to this than money. There's something that's of equal, or perhaps more value to me.

Not unreasonable: I don't think that's an unreasonable request. And if that's the only sticking point I won't let it stand in our way. We don't offer employment contracts but I think we can write up a simple letter between us that would suffice.

Negotiates: One month per year is pretty rich for us. It's going to be a real effort to get the people upstairs to agree to any kind of termination agreement. I'll need to speak with them and see what I can come up with. Can I tell them you've already accepted and that this is just a formality?

No can do: I understand your point of view and can sympathize. However the company has never given employment contracts and I don't think I'll be able to convince them to set a precedent for you. Is this a deal-breaker or are you interested in the job even without a termination agreement.

Offer thanks: I really appreciate your flexibility. That's just more proof that this is going to be a great place to work. I'm really looking forward to joining your team. When can I start?

Offer thanks: I realize my request is out of the ordinary and I appreciate anything and everything you could do on my behalf. With you going to bat for me I'm pleased to accept your offer of employment. When can I start?

Accept but . . . : I understand my request is out of the ordinary. It's certainly not a deal-breaker, but I'd appreciate it if you could become my advocate. Whether that comes through or not I'm delighted to accept your offer. When can I start?

219

Workscript 8.10 Negotiating a job offer when you're unemployed

Makes offer: *I'm very impressed with your qualifications and I think you're just the kind of person we're looking for. I'm offering you the position of department manager at a starting salary of $50,000. I know that's less than you were earning before, but the industry has changed and with the economy the way it is, that's the best we can do. What do you say?*

Thrilled...but: I'm thrilled at the possibility of coming to work here for you. And your salary offer won't stand in the way of accepting. My sole concern is trying to provide security for my family. I've had recent first-hand experience with how fickle the job market can be now. What I'd like is if we could agree as to what an appropriate severance package for termination without cause would be, prior to my coming aboard. Because of my family situation I'd like to know that I have at least one month's severance pay for every year I'm here.

220

Not unreasonable: *I don't think that's an unreasonable request. And if that's the only sticking point, I won't let it stand in our way. We don't offer employment contracts but I think we can write up a simple letter between us that would suffice.*

→ **Offer thanks:** *I really appreciate your flexibility. That's just more proof that this is going to be a great place to work. I'm really looking forward to joining your team. When can I start?*

Negotiates: *One month per year is pretty rich for us. It's going to be a real effort to get the people upstairs to agree to any kind of termination agreement. I'll need to speak with them and see what I can come up with. Can I tell them you've already accepted and that this is just a formality?*

→ **Offer thanks:** *I realize my request is out of the ordinary and I appreciate anything and everything you could do on my behalf. With your your going to bat for me, I'm pleased to accept your offer of employment. When can I start?*

No can do: *I understand your point of view and can sympathize. However, the company has never given employment contracts and I don't think I'll be able to convince them to set a precedent for you. Is this a deal-breaker or are you interested in the job even without a termination agreement?*

→ **Accept but . . . :** *I understand my request is out of the ordinary. It's certainly not a deal-breaker, but I'd appreciate it if you could become my advocate. Whether that comes through or not, I'm delighted to accept your offer. When can I start?*

Workscript 8.11 Giving notice

Break the news: *I've received an irresistible job offer from Acme, Inc., which I've accepted. They want me to start by the beginning of next month. I've come up with a transition plan that can help make my departure as smooth as possible. I think it should take no more than two weeks. If it takes less, I'll leave early, and if it takes more, I'll make myself available for consultation and guidance.*

Angry: *We don't need your help. Pack up your stuff and get out of here today. And don't even try to talk to your staff or call any of your clients. I'm going to call security to have them watch you don't steal anything and then escort you from the building.*

More time: *That's not enough time for us to make the transition. You might as well just leave today for all the good your plan is going to do me.*

Acceptance: *I hate to see you go, but that's part of business. Just make sure you finish your projects and have your transitions plan in place before you leave.*

Notice a mistake? Would you have preferred I just leave? I've told everyone in my department I was giving notice. If you throw me out today they'll see it would be a mistake for them to give notice. If you want me to leave today without helping ease the transition, that's fine with me. It's your choice.

→ **All I have:** I've given you as much time as I can and have offered everything I can to help out. If you'd prefer that I leave today and don't work on the transition, I will.

→ **Thanks:** I'll work as hard these two weeks as I ever have. Working for you has been a wonderful experience and I'm very grateful.

Backs off: *I should have realized hiring you was a mistake. Tie up any loose ends as fast as you can and then get out of here.*

→ **Backs off:** *No, I'm just upset. I'd appreciate your doing everything you can in the time remaining so we can avoid losing too much time and revenue.*

Today, the most important thing you can ask for in your initial negotiation is a termination agreement. We now know we're all temporary employees. Like baseball managers, we're hired to be fired. So the thing we truly lack is security. The prize to look for in your job negotiation is an agreement to pay you a certain amount in severance if (when) you are fired without cause. This needn't be an elaborately crafted agreement. A simple letter is fine. In fact, that's better since it won't require the involvement of attorneys.

If you're still employed when you engage in this negotiation, you have the flexibility to first make sure you'd be receiving market value for your services before pushing for the termination agreement. Your rationale for the request can be that you're giving up security and tenure to come to this new job, and need to maintain the safety net you've built before making the jump. See Workscript 8.9. Negotiating a job offer when you're still employed

If you're unemployed when you have this dialogue, insisting on market value pay shouldn't be a sticking point. Something is always better than nothing. Instead, you can immediately push for the termination agreement. In this case, your rationale can be that you have recent firsthand experience of how important it is to have plans for a soft landing in place. See Workscript 8.10.

Giving Notice

I don't think there's a more unbalanced interaction in the workplace than the process of giving notice. Think about it for a moment. An employer can fire with impunity, often not even letting someone who has provided decades of valuable service to the organization return to her desk and collect her personal belongings. There are many firms that have security guards escort employees out the door as if they were criminals. Yet employees are expected to give employers at least two weeks' notice of their impending departure.

That said, two wrongs don't make a right. And the people most often put in difficult positions by unplanned employee departures are the former coworkers, not the former employer. So despite the unfairness of it, I suggest you give at least two weeks' notice whenever you can. If the response is that you're immediately terminated, that's the employer's choice. You're not giving notice out of gratitude, but because you want to be magnanimous, be as supportive as you can to your coworkers, and maintain your reputation within the industry.

Rather than specify a time-frame when giving notice, I'd suggest you instead present a departure plan. Offer up your ideas on how you can help smooth the transition, and give an estimate of how long it will take. You can suggest that if it takes less time you'll leave early, and if it takes longer you'll try to remain available for consultation while at your new job. Simply say your new company needs you by such and such a date, and then present your transition plan.

Don't put up with any abuse: You've got another job already lined up. Say that your poor treatment will be a signal to others that giving notice is a mistake. See Workscript 8.11.

Epilogue

Providing a practical guide to problematic conversations in today's job market has led me to wonder if there's anything that we, as individuals, could do to make the workplace a more just environment. Can we turn back the clock to a time when employees were valued, when handshake deals were common, when if you did your work your position was secure—and if you did it well you'd be given raises and promotions? The simple, honest answer is *no*. Those days are gone and no matter how nostalgic some of us might be, they're never coming back. The hands of time move in only one direction: forward.

So what we need is to find a more just way of working in this new world. I don't think I've got the whole answer, but I do have a good place for us to start.

Rather than viewing ourselves as employees, subservient to those who sign our paychecks, what if we look at ourselves as freelancers who just happen to have one client. When we're hired, it's to accomplish a goal or deliver a product. We're working, not at a job, but on a project. Our employer is our client: someone to be respected, catered to, and helped; but not to be viewed as someone who is our source of long-term security. Instead of relying on our boss to provide for us, we need to provide for ourselves. That means constantly looking for more clients, expanding our offerings, and freshening our inventory of skills. It means accepting that once the project is done, we'll need to find work elsewhere.

Many individuals who have had the opportunity to "go freelance" over the years have shied away from it. Ironically, considering the current environment, people who've hesitated to freelance have always cited the lack of security and stability. The world of regular employment, as we now know it, is actually no more stable or secure than the freelancer's life. In fact, it's the freelancers who have more security today than the employees.

That's because they've learned how to provide fully satisfactory service to one client while actively looking for another. They're comfortable pitching themselves as the immediate solution to finite problems rather than as the long-term answer to unforeseen issues. They're always thinking outside the box about ways they could find new work and places they could mine for new business leads. Having learned to be self-reliant, freelancers are comfortable making economic and lifestyle adjustments.

In the coming years, perhaps the most important workscript of all will be the one in which you convince yourself that you can take charge of your own life. I'd love to help you with that conversation, too.

Stephen M. Pollan

Index

A

Acceptance letters, severance packages and, 50
Ad hoc workplace, general changes in, 8–10
Advancement, no guarantees of, 8
Age discrimination, company icon being fired and, 40
Alcohol problems:
  confronting employee with, workscript, 184–185
  dealing with, 182, 188
Anger, 9
  absorbing after breaking bad news, workscript, 145
  channeling, being terminated close to retirement and, 54
  minimizing, relocations and, 33
Annual reviews:
  changed nature of, 197
  future potential terminations and, 197, 199, 202
  manager and, 198
  in the past, 196
  scheduling of, 198–199
Anonymity, collective, ending backstabbing and, 159
Antagonistic relationships at work, 151
Appeals, 63

Appearance improvements:
  asking for, 152–153
  asking for, workscript, 154–155
Assignments
  turning down, 132–133
  turning down, workscript, 134–135
Attire, professional, 152–153
Authority challenges, avoiding, 62–63
Automatic raises, as thing of the past, 108
Availability, ongoing, of terminated employee, 55, 60–61, 64–65

B

Backhanded self-criticism, calling employee on, 202
Backstabbing:
  confronting someone engaging in, workscript, 162–163
  ending, 157, 159
  pay cuts and, preventing, 81
  privately putting end to, workscript, 160–161
  publicly putting an end to, workscript, 158
  standing out from the crowd and, 131
  verifying complaints related to, 157, 159

INDEX

Bad news, breaking, 142–143
Benefits packages:
    cutbacks and, maintenance of, 69
    negotiating job offers and, 213
    purchases/mergers and, 28
    turning into part-timer, workscript, 78–79
Bereaved employees, vacation time use and, 123, 130
"Blaming the messenger," warning of potential client or customer problems and, 143
Body language, 8
Body odor/hygiene problems, speaking with employee about, 153, 156
Bonus payments. *See* Cash bonuses
Boss:
    backstabbing aimed at, 157
    being nonthreatening to, 132
    breaking bad news to, 142–143
    breaking bad news to, workscript, 144–145
    encouraging prominence for, 131–132
Breaking bad news:
    to boss, 142–143
    to boss, workscript, 144–145
Breath mints, 153, 156
Bridging, as part of severance packages, 49, 53
Brownnosing:
    putting end to, 171
    putting end to, workscript, 174
Budget increase requests, 120, 122–123
    making, workscript, 126–127
    responding to, workscript, 124–125
    timing of, 123
Budget reductions:
    mandating from departments and teams, 102
    workscript, 103
Bureaucracy, reorganizations and, 26
Business attire, for meeting new staff, 20

C

Career model, traditional, collapse of, 7–8
Careers, expiration dates for, 3, 4–5, 70
Career shifts:
    selling to interviewer, 212–213
    selling to interviewer, workscript, 216–217
Cash bonuses:
    one-time, 107, 110
    one-time, in lieu of promotion, 115
    one-time, in lieu of promotion, workscript, 118, 121
    one-time, responding to raise request and, workscript, 113
Cash flow crises, furloughs without pay and, 71–73
Chain of command, making end run around your boss, workscript, 66–67
Chaos, in workplace, 13
Client problems:
    potential, warning of, 143, 150
    potential, warning of, workscript, 146–147
Clients:
    appearances and interactions with, 152
    constantly seeking new ones, 228
    relocations and, 31
Clothing choices, for meeting new staff, 20
COBRA coverage, severance packages and, 38, 43, 47, 53, 54, 56, 57, 58
Company icon:
    being terminated, workscript for, 44
    framing departure of, 40, 43, 44
    job no longer exists, workscript, 44
    legal leverage of, in face of termination, 40
    terminating, 38–41
    terminating, workscript, 42–43
    termination agreement terms and, 41
Company-wide pay cuts, 81, 84
Compassion, lack of, in today's termination process, 36

Index   231

Compensation, stock performance and, 5
Competitors, poaching key people from, 111
Compliments, excessive, confronting employee about, 171
Condolences, death in the family and, workscript, 128
Confidentiality:
  drying out drinking and, 182
  ending backstabbing and, 159
"Consulting" arrangements, for terminated employees asked to remain available, 61, 65
Contact lists, renting, 211–212
Continuing education expenses, 198
Corporate loyalty, death of, 6
Cost cutting, 106
Cost of living, relocations and, 31
Counteroffers, to pay raise requests, 109
Covering up for a peer:
  issues related to, 165
  refusing, workscript, 170
Covert backstabbing attacks, dealing with, 157
Coworkers, giving notice and, 225
Criticism:
  addressing, at performance review, 200, 201, 202
  defending your own performance from, workscript, 201
Customer problems:
  potential, warning of, 143, 150
  potential, warning of, workscript, 146–147
Customers:
  appearances and interactions with, 152
  termination of company icon and, 39
Customer service skills:
  critical performance review and, workscript, 200
  improving your job security and, workscript, 201
Cut-backs, 69
Cutting costs, 106

D

Dates, being asked out on, workscript, 179
Deadline extensions:
  asking for, 137, 142
  asking for, workscript, 140–141
Death in the family:
  responding to time off request, workscript, 128–129
  time off request and, 123, 130
Deferring termination, 64–65
Deflating expenses, 192, 194
Departments:
  budget reductions from, 102
  handling raise requests and dynamics in, 110
  pay cuts across, 81
  promotion requests and, 115
Departure plans, presenting, 225
Departures:
  framing for terminated employees asked to remain available, 55
  two weeks' notice and, 224–225
Direct reporters, meeting, 20
Disabled dependent, terminating someone with, 49, 54
Discrimination, wrongful termination suits and, 40
Dissension, minimizing chances of, 71
Documentation, 9. *See also* Memos
Double entendres, 171
Dressing professionally, 152–153
Drinking problems:
  confronting employee with, workscript, 184–185
  confronting peer with, 182
  confronting peer with, workscript, 186–187
Drug problems, dealing with, 182

E

Educational courses:
  responding to requests for self-criticism and need for, workscript, 206–207
  self-criticism during annual review and request for, 202

INDEX

Effusiveness, as counterproductive, 15, 16
Electronic communication, face-to-face communication as rarity and, 3–4
Electronic tracking, of employee Internet use, 188
"Elevator" version of new boss presentation, 17
Embezzlement, 188
Emergency job protection, workscript, 82–83
Empathy, lack of, in today's termination process, 36
Employee appreciation, one-time bonus payments and, 106
Employee budgets, reducing, workscript, 100–101
Employee expenses, questioning, workscript, 190–191
Employee extortion, examples of, 107
Employee goal-setting, manager's image and, 198
Employee replacement costs, 106
Employee requests:
 in difficult economic environment, 105
 fall-back strategies for, 106–107
 for raises, 108–111, 114
Employees:
 asking for self-criticism, workscript, 204–205
 asking sacrifices of, 69
 distrust of employers by, 6, 9
 ending backstabbing among, 157–159
 expendability of, 36
 flirtatious, 171, 175, 178
 judging on short-term results, 5
 toxic relationship between management and, 36
Employee security, freelancer's security vs., 228
Employer cost-cutting, 69–103
 budget reductions, 102
 expanding responsibility without increasing pay, 85, 89

full-time jobs becoming part-time jobs, 73, 77
furloughs without pay, 71–73
increasing hours but not pay, 85
pay cuts, 81, 84–85
staff reductions, 95, 98
Employer-provided benefits, negotiating job offers and, 213. *See also* Benefits packages
Employers, employees' distrust of, 6. *See also* Boss; Managing up
Employment:
 annual reviews and transitory nature of, 198
 changing terms of, 70
End runs:
 making, 62–63, 73
 making, workscript, 66–67
Excellent employees, annual review of, 202–203
Executive evaluations, stock performance and, 5
Expanded roles, promotion requests and, workscript, 118–119
Expanded work hours without expanded pay, workscript, 90–91
Expendability, of employees, 36
Expense reports:
 defending your own, 192
 defending your own, workscript, 193
 deflating expenses, 192
 questioning, workscript, 190–191
Expenses, deflating, 192, 194
Expense trimming, pay cuts and, 81, 84–85
Eye contact:
 employee requests and, 107
 promotion requests and, 120

F

Face-to-face communication:
 between individuals who don't know each other, 9
 performance reviews and, 197
 as a rarity in today's workplace, 3–4, 70, 151

Index

termination process and rarity of, 36
Fall-back strategies, to employee requests, 106–107
Family emergencies, 123, 130
Family needs, severance package for someone with, 56, 57, 58
Fashion statements, workplace and, 152–153
Favoritism:
  relocations and sense of, 32
  staff reductions and, 95
Fearful supervisors, standing out from the crowd and, 131
Fears, 9
  acknowledging, meeting new staff and, 21
  channeling, being terminated close to retirement and, 54
Firings, 8. *See also* Terminations
  of company icon, 38–41
  frequency of, 35
  friends firing friends, 41, 45
  friends firing friends, workscripts, 46–47, 48
  on Mondays, 98
Flattery:
  extravagant, public nature of, 171
  putting an end to, workscript, 174
Flex-time arrangements:
  pay cuts and, 84, 88
  valued employees and, 109, 112
Flight risk, 107, 111
Flirtations, 152
  stopping, 171, 175, 178
  stopping, workscript, 176–177
Flirtatious peer, stopping, workscript, 179
Freelancers, security of, 228
Freezing costs, 106
Friends:
  being fired by, 41, 45
  being fired by, workscript, 48
Full time employee, turning into part-timer, workscript, 78–79
Full-time jobs, turning into part-time jobs, 73, 77

Furloughs without pay:
  issues related to, 71–73
  workscript, 74–75
Furloughs with pay, employee viewpoint, workscript, 76

G

Giving notice:
  issues related to, 195, 224–225
  workscript, 222–223
Globalization, job eliminations and, 5
Good ideas, remaining open to, 106
Gossip, 8, 152
  restructuring and, 24
  silencing, 178, 182
  silencing, workscript, 180–181
  termination of company icon and, 39
Gossips, confronting, workscript, 183–184
Government programs, benefit packages and, 213
Great Depression, 7
Great Recession of 2008:
  collapse of traditional career model and, 7–8
  lack of reward for high performance and, 6–7
  workplace transformation and, 1, 3
Group introduction, for meeting new staff, 20
Group meetings, company-wide pay cuts and, 81
Group settings, transition conversations in, 15–16

H

Health coverage, terminations close to retirement and, 49, 54. *See also* COBRA coverage
High performing employees, Great Recession of 2008 and impact on, 6–7
Hit lists, flight risks and, 111
Honesty, 15, 16
Hours increased, without pay increase, 85

234 INDEX

Human resources representatives, at termination meetings, 39, 49
Hygiene problems:
  asking for improvements in, 153
  asking for improvements in, workscript, 156

I

Income, knowledge, increased skill and upward climb in, 7, 8
Individual pay cuts:
  private communication about, 84
  workscript, 86–87
Industry associations, staying active in, 211
Industry observers, termination of company icon and, 39
Industry shifts, as norm in current work environment, 212–213
Informational interviews, 211, 212
Information technology, elimination of jobs and, 4–5
Internet privilege abuse:
  ending, 188
  ending, workscript, 189
Interviewer:
  selling your career shift to, 212–213
  selling your career shift to, workscript, 216–217
Interviews:
  informational, 211, 212
  job, 195

J

Jealousy, meeting your new staff and, 22
Job elimination:
  globalization and, 5
  terminating company icon and, 40, 42–43, 44
Job extinction, robbing tomorrow for today and, 6
Job fishing, 211
Job hunting, when full-time job turns part-time, 73
Job interviews, 195

Job market, increasing your value in, 203
Job offers:
  negotiating, 213, 224
  negotiating, when you're still employed, workscript, 218–219
  negotiating while unemployed, workscript, 220–221
Job protection:
  emergency, workscript, 82–83
  relocations and, 30
Jobs:
  expiration dates for, 3, 4–5, 36, 70
  finite nature of, 9, 10
Job security:
  freelancers and, 228
  nonexistent, 133
Just workplace environment, self-reliance and, 227–228

L

Law suits, terminating someone with personal burden and, 54
Layoffs, industry- and profession-wide, 212–213
Legal exposure, minimizing, terminations close to retirement and, 49
Legal leverage:
  company icon being fired and, 40
  terminating someone with personal burden and reality of, 54
Legal liability of company:
  minimizing, terminations and, 37
  recommendations and, 63
Legislative environment, changed, terminations and, 197
Lifescripts (Pollan), 2, 10
Longevity, raise requests and, 112
Looking out for number one, 195–225
  giving notice, 224–225
  negotiating job offers, 213, 224
  performance reviews, 196–203
  renting a contact list, 211–212
  selling your career shift to an interviewer, 212–213
Loyalty, death of, 6

Index 235

M

Malicious personal attacks among staff, dealing with, workscript, 180–181
Management, toxic relationship between employees and, 36
Manager, annual reviews all about, 197, 198
Managerial decisions, all about the money, 14
Managing up, 131–150
  asking for relief from a project, 136–137, 138–139
  breaking bad news, 142–143, 144–145
  deadline extension requests, 137, 140–141
  turning down an assignment, 132–135
  warning of potential client or customer problems, 143, 146–147
  warning of potential vendor or supplier problems, 148–149, 150
Market value, salary raise requests in context of, 109, 110, 112, 203, 218
Mass firings, standardized severance packages and, 38
Medical coverage, terminating someone close to retirement and, 49, 54. *See also* COBRA coverage
"Meet and greet," in group setting, 20
Memos:
  budget increase requests and, 122
  drafting, meeting new boss and, 16–17
  requesting release from project and, 136
Mercenary motives, 195
Mergers:
  announcing, 24–25
  announcing, workscript, 28–29
Merit, pay raises no longer tied to, 213
Morale problems, 15, 16
  avoiding, 70
  termination of company icon and, 39
Moving, announcing, workscript, 30–31

N

Negotiating job offers, 213, 224
  when you're unemployed, workscript, 220–221
  while still employed, workscript, 218–219
Nepotism, staff reductions and, 95
Networking:
  scheduling weekly time for, 211
  social connections and, 211–212
Networking meetings:
  asking for, workscript, 214–215
  looking out for number one and, 195
New boss, meeting, 16–19
  primary goal in, 16
  workscript, 18–19
New hires, existing employees *vs.*, 106
New staff, meeting:
  issues related to, 20–21
  workscript, 22–23
New workplace environment, 1–11
  elements of, 3
  employees do not trust employers, 3, 6
  everyone's work future is uncertain, 3, 7–8
  face-to-face communication is rare, 3–4
  jobs and careers have expiration dates, 3, 4–5
  short-term results are all that matter, 3, 5–6
Nimbleness, in scripting, 9
Noncash rewards, for valued employees, 107
Nonemergencies, time off request, workscript, 128
Notice:
  full-time job becoming a part-time job and, 77
  giving, 224–225
  giving, workscript, 222–223

INDEX

O

Offerings, expanding, 228
Office behavior, ignoring all rules for, 1
Office supplies, petty theft of, 188
One-time cash bonuses, 107, 110
   in lieu of promotion, 115
   in lieu of promotion, workscript, 118–119, 121
   responding to raise request and, workscript, 112–113
Organizations, appearances and perceptions of, 152
Outplacement counseling, severance packages and, 38, 47
Outside offers:
   as leverage for raise, schedule issues, 114
   security guarantees and, 111
Overt backstabbing attacks, dealing with, 157

P

Part-time employee, being asked to become, workscript, 80
Part-time jobs, full-time jobs turning into, 73, 77
Past performance, promotion requests and, 114
Pay:
   extending responsibilities without increase in, 85, 89
   extending responsibilities without increase in, workscript, 92–93
   furloughs without, 71–73
   furloughs without, workscript, 74–75
   increasing hours without increase in, 85
Pay cuts, 81, 84–85
   company-wide, 81
   cutting an entire staff's pay, workscript, 82–83
   employees experiencing, workscript, 88
   individual, 84

Pay raises:
   performance reviews and, 196
   rarity of, 203, 213
Pensions, 7
Percentage goals, for budget reductions, 102
Performance reviews, 8, 195, 196–199, 202–203
   asking an employee for self-criticism, workscript, 204–205
   critical, delivering, workscript, 200
   defending your own performance from criticism, workscript, 201
   delivering critical, workscript, 200
   offering suggestions for professional development, workscript, 208–209
   responding to requests for self criticism, workscript, 206–207
   responding to suggestions for professional development, workscript, 210
   scheduling of, 198–199
Personal burden:
   terminating someone with, 49, 54
   terminating someone with, workscript, 56–57
Personal connections, networking and, 211–212
Personal days, 123
Personal emergencies, time off requests for, 130
Personal finances, furloughs without pay and, 72
Personal history, paucity of, at workplace, 9
Personal rapport, unimportant role of, 14
Personal savings, 7
Personnel cuts, meeting new staff and timing of, 21
Personnel experts, at termination meetings, 39, 49
Petty theft, 188
Phased-in pay cuts, 84
Pilferage, 188
Pirated computer files, downloading at work, 188

Index

Politeness, 15, 16
Political costs, promotion requests and, 115
Pornography, browsing at work, 188
Power, sexual harassment and, 164
Praise, for excellent employee at annual review, 202–203
Preemptive action, potential vendor or supplier problems and, 150
Producers, number-one, 132
Professional development:
  offering suggestions for, workscript, 208–209
  responding to suggestions for, workscript, 210
Professionalism, supremacy of, 14
Professional organizations, staying active in, 211
Profession-wide layoffs, 212–213
Projects:
  asking for release from, 136–137
  asking for release from, workscript, 138–139
  talking to boss about, 132
Prominence, not striving for, 131
Promotion requests, 114–115, 120
  making, workscript, 121
  responding to, workscript, 118–119
  timing of, 120
Propaganda, avoiding, meeting new staff and, 20
Purchase:
  announcing, 24–25
  announcing, workscript, 28–29

Q

Quality, employee budget cuts and, 100
Quid pro quo arrangements, for terminated employees asked to remain available, 55

R

Raise requests, 8, 108–111, 114
  alternatives to, 109–110
  responding to, workscript, 112–113
  workscript, 116–117
Raises, rarity of, 203, 213

Ratting out a peer:
  issues related to, 165
  workscript, 172–173
Real estate sales, relocations and, 32
Realism, 15
Recommendations, liability issues and, 63
Regulatory environment, changed, terminations and, 197
Reinstatement, forgetting about, 37–38
Release from a project:
  asking for, 136–137
  asking for, workscript, 138–139
Relief effect, taking advantage of, 70
Relocation:
  announcing, 25, 32–33
  announcing, workscript, 30–31
Rental assistance, relocations and, 30
Renting contact lists, 211–212
Reparation action, breaking bad news and, 143
Replacement tactic, employee requests and, 106
Reputation, requesting release from project and, 136
Requesting release from project, suggesting replacements and, 137
Resignations:
  of terminated employees asked to remain available, 55
  terminating company icon and, 40
Responsibilities:
  expanding without pay increase, 85, 89
  expanding without pay increase, workscript, 92–93, 94
Restrictive covenants, in termination agreements, 41
Restructuring:
  explaining, 21, 24
  explaining, workscript, 26–27
Resume, 211
Retirement:
  being terminated when close to, workscript, 52–53

Retirement: *(continued)*
  terminating someone close to, 45, 49
  terminating someone close to, workscript, 50–51
Retirement plans, purchases/mergers and, 28
Retraining in another field, severance package for company icon and, 44
Return dates, furloughs without pay and, 71
Reversals, winning, 62–63
Rumors, dealing with, workscript, 180–181. *See also* Gossip

S

Sacrifices, employee, lack of workplace trust and, 69, 70
Salaries, performance reviews and, 196
Salary negotiations, 195
Salary raises, rarity of, 203, 213
Salary range, raise requests and, 108
Salary reviews, canceling, 83
Sales, budget reductions and, 102
School registrations, relocations and, 32
Security guarantees, outside offers and, 111
Security guards, employees escorted out the door by, 224–225
Self-criticism:
  asking employee for, workscript, 204–205
  asking for, at performance review, 202
  responding to requests for, workscript, 206–207
Self-reliance, necessity of, in new work world, 228
Seniority, 7
  bridging, being terminated when close to retirement, workscript, 52–53
  company icon being fired and, 40
Sensitivity, lack of, in today's termination process, 36

Severance packages:
  "bridging" as part of, 49, 53
  company icon and, 40, 41, 42, 44
  company icon and, workscript, 42–43
  documenting, 36
  friends firing friends and, 45, 48
  full-time job becoming a part-time job and, 77
  relocations and, 30, 32
  standardized, 38
  for terminating employee and asking them to remain available, 55
  for terminating employee close to retirement, workscript, 50–51, 52
  for terminating employee with personal burden, workscript, 56, 57, 58–59
  when full-time job turns part-time, 73
Severance ranges, staff reductions and, 98
Sexual harasser:
  confronting, 164
  confronting, workscript, 166–167
Sexual harassment:
  accusations of, 175
  ending, 159, 164
  ending, workscript, 168–169
  third party accusations and, 164
Share prices, short-term results and, 5
Short-term performance, primacy of, 3, 5–6, 9, 36
Short-term results, career shifts and, 213
Sick days, 123
Sick dependent, terminating someone with, 49, 54
Silencing gossip, 178, 182
Skepticism, 9
Skills, freshening, 228
Slander, public rebuke of, workscript, 160–161
Slovenly dress, 152
Social capital, networking and, 211–212
Social Security, 7

Index 239

Special needs, relocations and, 31
Spending, trimming, 102
Spin, avoiding, meeting new staff and, 20
Staff, meeting new, 20–21
Staff backstabbing:
   dealing with, 157, 159
   privately putting end to, workscript, 160–161
   putting an end to, indirect private approach, workscript, 158
Staff reductions:
   having your staff cut, workscript, 99
   issues related to, 95, 98
   in wake of purchase or merger, 24, 25
   workscript, 96–97
Stock performance, short-term results and, 5
Substance abuse problems, dealing with, 182
Success, striving for, 131
Supplier problems:
   potential, warning of, 150
   potential, warning of, workscript, 148–149
Suppliers, termination of company icon and, 39
Surgery, time off request, workscript, 128–129

T

Team dynamics, handling raise requests and, 110
Teams, budget reductions from, 102
Teamwork, signaling importance of, 20
Telecommuting arrangements:
   as alternative to raises, 109
   relocations and, 31
   for valued employees, 112
Tension, in new workplace, 9
Tenure, pay raises no longer tied to, 213
Termination agreements, 116, 117, 196
   importance of, 224
   negotiating job offer while still employed and, 218, 219, 224
   negotiating job offer while unemployed and, 220–221, 224
Termination letter, employee with personal burden and, 56, 57, 58
Termination meeting, formal script and, 37
Terminations, 13. *See also* Firings
   approaching in humane way, 37
   asking employee to remain available after, 55, 60–61, 64–65
   of company icon, 38–41
   of company icon, workscript, 42–43
   deferring, 62, 64–65
   frequency of, 35
   friends firing friends, 41, 45
   new reasons for problematic nature of, 197
   of someone close to retirement, 45, 49
   of someone close to retirement, workscript, 50–51, 52–53
   of someone with personal burden, 49, 54
   of someone with personal burden, workscript, 56–57
   when you have a personal burden, workscript, 58–59
Theft, 188
Time off requests, 123, 130
   relocations and, 30
   responding to, workscript, 128–129
Title improvements:
   as alternative to raise, 110
   as alternative to raise, workscript, 112–113
Training:
   for excellent employees, 203
   responding to requests for self-criticism and need for, workscript, 206–207
   self-criticism during annual review and request for, 202
Training budget, professional development costs and, workscript, 208–209
Training expenses, 198

INDEX

Transition conversations, in group settings, 15–16
Transition plans:
  giving notice and, 222–223
  presenting, 225
Trends in workplace, staying in touch with, 211
Trust, 15
  employee sacrifices and lack of, 69, 70
  lack of, between employees and employers, 6, 9
  performance reviews and lack of, 197
  raise requests and, 111
  today's workplace and reasons for lack of, 36
Turning down assignments, 132–133
  timing discussion about, 133
  workscript, 134–135
Two weeks' notice, 224–225

U

Uncertainty:
  explaining restructuring and, 21, 24
  of work future, 7–8
Unemployment:
  inability to accept change and, 70
  negotiating job offer during, 220–221
Unemployment benefits, filing for, 98
Unfair terminations, employees with some protection against, 197
Unpredictability, in workplace, 13

V

Vacation time:
  bereaved employee and, 123, 130
  giving up, in exchange for furlough without pay, 72
Valued employees:
  keeping, 107
  responding to raise requests from, workscript, 112–113
Vendor problems:
  potential, warning of, 150
  potential, warning of, workscript, 148–149
Vendors:
  employee budget cuts and, 100
  employees taking over tasks sent to, 109
  stop farming work out to, 85, 89
  termination of company icon and, 39
Verification, 9
Verifying backstabbing complaints, 157, 159
Vesting, terminations of someone close to retirement and, 50–51, 52
Vulnerability, termination of company icon and, 39

W

Wardrobe choices, 20, 152–153
Work future, uncertainty of, 7–8
Workplace, unpredictability in, 13
Workplace bombshells, importance of, 13–14
Work project issues, talking to boss about, 132
Workscripts:
  asking employee for self-criticism, 204–205
  asking for improved appearance, 154–155
  asking for improved hygiene, 156
  asking for networking meeting, 214–215
  asking for relief from a project, 138–139
  being asked to become part-time employee, 80
  being fired by a friend, 48
  being furloughed without pay, 76
  being terminated, but asked to remain available, 64–65
  being terminated when close to retirement, 52–53
  being terminated when you have a personal burden, 58–59
  breaking bad news to your boss, 144–145

Index

confronting a gossip, 183–184
confronting a sexual harasser, 166
confronting employee with drinking problem, 184–185
confronting peer with drinking problem, 186–187
confronting someone who's backstabbing you, 162–163
cutting an entire staff's pay, 82–83
cutting an individual employee's pay, 86
deadline extension requests, 140–141
defending your own expense report, 193
defending your own performance from criticism, 201
delivering a critical performance review, 200
ending Internet privilege abuse, 189
ending staff sexual harassment, 168–169
expanded work hours without expanded pay, 90–91
explaining a restructuring, 26–27
explaining career shift to interviewer, 216–217
firing a friend, 46–47
furloughing someone without pay, 74–75
giving notice, 222–223
having your budget reduced, 103
having your pay cut, 88
having your responsibilities increased but not your pay, 94
having your staff cut, 99
icon being terminated, 44
increasing employee's hours but not pay, 90
individual pay cuts, 86–87
making end run around your boss, 66–67
meeting your new boss, 18–19
meeting your new staff, 22–23
negotiating job offer when you're still employed, 218–219
negotiating job offer when you're unemployed, 220–221
offering suggestions for professional development, 208–209
privately putting an end to staff backstabbing, 160–161
publicly putting an end to staff backstabbing, 158
purchase or merger announcement, 28–29
putting an end to brownnosing, 174
putting end to staff gossiping, 180–181
questioning employee expenses, 190–191
ratting out a peer, 172–173
reducing employee's budget, 100–101
reducing employee's staff, 96–97
refusing to cover up for a peer, 170
relocation announcement, 30–31
requesting a budget increase, 126–127
requesting a promotion, 121
requesting a raise, 116–117
responding to a promotion request, 118–119
responding to budget increase request, 124–125
responding to raise request, 112–113
responding to request for time off, 128–129
responding to requests for self-criticism, 206–207
responding to suggestions for professional development, 210
stopping a flirtatious employee, 176–177
stopping a flirtatious peer, 179
terminating company icon, 42–43
terminating someone, but asking them to remain available, 60–61
terminating someone close to retirement, 50–51
terminating someone with personal burden, 56–57

Workscripts: *(continued)*
   turning down an assignment, 134–135
   turning full time employee into a part-timer, 78–79
   warning of potential client or customer problems, 146–147
   warning of potential vendor or supplier problems, 148–149
   you're the icon being terminated, 44
Work team leaders, staff reductions and, 95, 98
World War II, 7
Wrongful termination suits:
   firing an icon and, 40
   increasing severance package and, 49